MEMO

OF AN

OLD CAMPDONIAN

By F. W. Coldicott

To Liz,
With very
Best Wishes, and
all my Love x x x

The Author
c. 1914

F. W. Coldicott.

Edited by Craig Fees

Cover painting by the Author

Campden and District Historical and Archæological Society
Chipping Campden, Gloucestershire
1994

To Mum
Many happy returns of the day.
19 August 1994.
With lots, lots of love
Maureen. x x x

Published by
**CAMPDEN & DISTRICT
HISTORICAL AND ARCHÆOLOGICAL SOCIETY**
Chipping Campden, Gloucestershire

©1994 The Author

ISBN 0-9511434-2-5

Printed in England by The Vale Press Ltd

FOREWORD
by the
Hon. Gerard Noel

It is a great honour to have been asked to write this short Foreword to the Campden memories of Fred Coldicott, made possible through the enterprise of the Campden and District Historical and Archaeological Society.

It so happens that before Fred knew about the Society's plans, he had lent me another copy of these same Memories, which I read with great interest. They represent, indeed, a uniquely valuable, living record of twentieth century life in our own, much loved, Cotswold town, by one of its most prominent and popular senior citizens.

So interesting was it, that I approached Fred about arranging for the appearance of his story in combination with recollections, which I had undertaken to collect, of certain other senior Campdonians, the whole to be published in a single volume together with selected photographs. This plan was pre-empted by the admirable initiative of the Historical Society, with the splendid result now available for all of us to see and admire.

I have had the privilege of knowing Fred nearly all my life, having already got to know his first wife Millie (Clifton) when I was only about ten! What a thrill, therefore, to be associated, in however small a way, with this delightful publication, in which an old and valued friend tells so vividly and faithfully his own tale of a long and eventful life in the town we both love so much.

We are greatly in the debt not only of the Campden Historical Society but also, in a very special way, of Dr. Craig Fees for the painstaking and scholarly fashion in which he has introduced and edited Fred's typescript.

I do not, moreover, in this context, use the word "scholarly" without good reason, for there is probably no one who knows more about Campden history than Dr. Fees. He has compiled a "bibliography" - though it is really even more than that - not only of standard works about Campden but also of virtually every important reference thereto in other published works.

Who better to have so kindly undertaken the preparation and presentation of Fred's wonderful account of the people and events he remembers so well during a lifetime in the one and only Chipping Campden!

The result is not just a memorial of Chipping Campden by Fred Coldicott. It is also, even more importantly, a memorial of Fred Coldicott by Chipping Campden. I can think of nothing more appropriate and timely, and welcome this happy publishing event with all my heart.

- Gerard Noel

CONTENTS

ILLUSTRATIONS

Front cover painting by the Author

Photographs
From the Author's collection, except where noted by an asterix,
for which see Acknowledgements..

Maps

"Mother visiting Mrs. Green's house, about 1908."

EDITOR'S INTRODUCTION

Chipping Campden, the historic capital of the North Cotswolds, on the northern boundary of Gloucestershire, is one of the most famous rural towns in England. It has been the setting for countless films and television shows. Its old buildings appear regularly on magazine covers and in travel brochures. It has been home to many well-known artists and writers - novelist Graham Greene, artist/engraver F.L. Griggs, designer Sir Gordon Russell, stained-glass artist Paul Woodroffe, composer Joseph Moorat. It has been praised by Lewis Carroll, sketched by John Rennie MacKintosh, toured by George Bernard Shaw, addressed by J.R.R. Tolkien, graced by the presence of royalty. It also played host to one of the most ambitious social experiments of this century: the move of 150 men, women and children, and the workshops of the Guild of Handicraft from the East End of London to Chipping Campden in 1902, as celebrated in Alan Crawford's award-winning C.R. Ashbee: Architect, Designer and Romantic Socialist (Yale University Press, 1985), and Fiona MacCarthy's The Simple Life: C.R. Ashbee in the Cotswolds (Lund Humphries, 1981). The town and its history feature in doctoral dissertations and masters' theses, dozens of books and literally hundreds (if not thousands) of articles, popular and academic.

This is the first time, however, that the story of 20th century Campden has been told by someone born and bred in the town. Indeed, I know of only two other books about Campden which have been written by local people: Josephine Griffiths's Chipping Campden: Today and Yesterday, published in 1931; and Jack Horne's Chipping Campden From the Grassroots published privately in 1982. Both are well worth reading, but neither weaves together history and personal experience as Mr. Coldicott does, illuminating this beautiful and celebrated town from the inside, as it were, for the first time. Some who thought they knew Chipping Campden will be surprised by what they find here. Others, coming to Campden for the first time through this book, will experience a sense of recognition and a deepening understanding of rural England.

THE AUTHOR

Mr. Coldicott was born in 1910 in the house next to what is now the County Library in the High Street, and apart from military service during World War II has lived his entire life in the town. He is related to farming families throughout the Vale of Evesham and the Cotswolds. He is cousin to the Campden Izods whose ancestors erected the famous Four

vii

Cross Hands finger-post on the main Broadway to Oxford Road in 1669, and cousin to the Haines who were among the most powerful farmers in Campden at the turn of the century, and farm there still. He started work at fourteen first for his father on the land and then as a labourer, graduated by chance to become lorry driver for a local builder, by good fortune and judgement trained as and became a mason at the end of World War II, and finally, with his friend Val Hobbs, and with the help of Lord and Lady Gainsborough, established his own firm of local builders in 1968. He retired in 1979.

CAMPDEN'S RECENT HISTORY: B.G. (Before the Guild)

The story of Campden which goes on within and behind Mr. Coldicott's narrative is one of extraordinary social and economic change. It began in one sense with the industrial revolution and the progressive shifting of the weight of public life and culture from rural England to its cities during the 19th century. As far as Campden is concerned it can probably be traced more specifically to the great Agricultural Depression which began in the late 1870s, and the crisis in local life which it brought on. Campden was an agricultural town, the centre of a reasonably prosperous agricultural district: Her economy and her social and political life turned on farming. Consequently, when the Agricultural Depression hit, it was devastating: Between the censuses of 1871 and 1901 the town lost nearly a quarter of its population - not just the agricultural labourers and the maids, going elsewhere to try to find work, but the middle classes whose homes and businesses employed so many women and men and kept local shops and growers in prosperity.

By the 1880s there was no question that the local economy and local life were in danger of cycling into fundamental decline, and that something had to be done to create jobs and to attract and to hold people in the town. That something would now be called tourism, and in the 1880s and 1890s people in Campden and outsiders with a personal and financial interest there (such as Percy Rushen, absentee landlord and author of The History and Antiquities of Chipping Campden, first published by the author in 1899) made a concerted effort to attract visitors, summer residents, group tours and conferences. The town was cleaned and trimmed and publicised, and in general terms the effort was a success. Campden is undoubtedly one of the most beautiful towns in England, and around the turn of the century, in a process that began to pick up pace in the 1920s and 1930s and has snowballed since the 1960s, Campden was "discovered" by the press and by people of influence, such as architect E. Guy Dawber and writer Laurence Housman. Increasing numbers visited, and increasing numbers decided it was a place in which they would like to live. The centre of the local economy began its gradual shift from agriculture towards what would today be called the leisure industry.

CAMPDEN'S RECENT HISTORY: THE GUILD OF HANDICRAFT

The single greatest "discovery" of Campden was that made by the Guild of Handicraft in 1902. The Guild of Handicraft was a company of Art and Craft workshops founded in the East End of London in 1888. It had developed from a class devoted to the ideas of John Ruskin and William Morris which had been led by visionary architect/designer C.R. Ashbee. Ashbee - who remained the director of and main spokesman for the Guild throughout its history - saw the Guild as a social and educational tool through which the living and working world of the British workman could be humanised and revolutionised, and the British Empire thereby revitalised from within. Founded on Guild Socialist principles, the men had a say in the running of the company, were encouraged to mingle, learn from and work with their fellow Guildsmen in the other workshops (silversmiths with woodworkers, jewellery makers with blacksmiths, bookbinders with printers), and were encouraged to develop and exploit an ethos of shared, self-improving leisure - plays, sports, educational travel.

Out of this vision came the idea of moving the men and the workshops from the soul-destroying, mechanistic City to the beautiful, history-rich and healthful surroundings of the Country, where creativity, community, and the hand-based skills of the Guildsmen could blossom. Just before Christmas 1901 the majority of the men in the London workshops voted to move to Chipping Campden, and in the Spring of 1902 the men and their families and tools began to arrive. There were some 150 of them, counting wives and children, and they represented one in ten of the population of Campden. So profound was their impact that the recent history of Campden continues to be dated from their coming.

For a variety of reasons the Guild as a commercial enterprise did not flourish after the move to Campden; indeed, profits declined and as it moved towards bankruptcy the company itself was wound up, in 1907/1908. Most of the workmen and their families then left Campden, but a sizeable rump remained, and while pursuing individual careers they continued to pursue the Guild's fundamentally liberal, artistic and educational aims within the town. Indeed, this "rump" formed a nucleus for a growing community of like-minded newcomers, some of whom

ix

had been attracted to the area by the Guild. Elements and successors of the Guild and of this community can be found in the town to this day, and appear regularly in Mr. Coldicott's Memories.

CAMPDEN'S RECENT HISTORY: A.G. (After the Guild)

The upheavals which followed the coming of the Guild to Campden can perhaps be imagined. In an agricultural town run largely by Conservatives, however progressive, a set of workshops run on socialist lines and sincerely believing they were pioneering the aesthetic, intellectual and industrial shape of the future, did not sit entirely easily. At the same time, the Guild was undeniably an economic asset, both in its own right, and because it attracted internationally-known artists and thinkers, and lesser known idealists - cultural tourists - who brought money in and spread the message of Campden abroad. The town, which was already known, benefitted greatly from the publicity generated by the Guild.

Inevitably, however, as the area became better known it also became a place in which more and more people wanted to live, or at least to have homes. Up to a point this is precisely what people in the town had been aiming to achieve. Past that point the balance changed. Rents which had gone up with the coming of the well-paid Guildsmen, displacing a small number of labourers who could not meet the new rent, continued to rise. Property prices entered an accelerating upward spiral, and between the wars local surveyors watched in surprise as the prices people were willing to pay for houses in the area skyrocketed. Outsiders coming in escalated pressures for amenities they were used to taking for granted in their cities and suburbs: continuous supplies of piped water, sewers, electricity, roads paved to take cars. Ideas about how the town should look took on a political dimension, as newer residents and visitors argued among themselves over issues of change and development from which many Campden people began to feel themselves excluded.

With the shift in balance of economic and social weight from local to newcomer, an increasing number of local people began to find themselves displaced from the heart of Campden, both physically and politically. It is a process which can be seen clearly between the wars, but it began to pick up momentum after World War II, and in the late 60s and early 70s local people began to talk openly and seriously of the extinction of the Campden native: With so many properties taken by people from outside, with property prices rising too high for young people starting out in married life to afford, and with fewer and fewer

X

"real" jobs in an increasingly tourist and leisure-based economy, it was wondered where the future generation of Campden children would come from. It was for this future generation that Mr. Coldicott began writing his Memories, and for whom he originally set out to describe the Campden in which he was born and in which he was raised.

*

Campden and the world have changed dramatically in the time covered by Mr. Coldicott's memories. All of this appears in the book, thrown up in the matter-of-fact way that a life is lived. Two of the former Guild cabinet makers teach schoolboy Fred Coldicott woodwork, one of whom, Jim Pyment, also gives him a lesson in practical jokesmanship. The firm of builders which Pyment built out of the collapse of the Guild later employs Mr. Coldicott and gives him his boost into the world of full-time, life-time work. Alec Miller, a sculptor who came to Campden with the Guild and stayed when the Guild broke up, employs Mr. Coldicott to take pieces to an exhibition in London, stopping off in Oxford to visit Miller's son. Artist F.L. Griggs, who pioneered the preservation movement in Campden between the wars, appears. Here are the first airplane, the first mains sewers, the coming of the telephone and the wireless (with its dance band broadcast from London): two world wars and all the many bringers and harbingers of change which have transformed Campden in the 20th century. It was the centre of its own agricultural district. It has become a satellite of the urban/international electronic economy, the centres of culture of which are diffused in cities around the world - in all of which Campden may be found in memories and in photographs in magazines and brochures promoting tourism to Britain. It is all here, quietly, like fragments of mirror, making up the history of the town as lived by one man, for whom the rhythm and the history of the town lie in the town's people and the things they did and that happened to them: the marriages, the haircuts, the insanity and the suicide, the narrow escapes and the practical jokes, and the crimes and courting and celebrations and fun which, for those who lived it, Campden was and is. It is a surprisingly candid book, with its story vividly told.

A NOTE ON THE TEXT

I met Mr. Coldicott in 1985 after giving a talk in the Town Hall. Dorrie Ellis pointed him out to me, and my initial reaction was frankly one of apprehension: I saw a towering man in an army greatcoat, in a town in which, as an outsider researching it, I tended to feel myself intruding at the best of times. Had Mrs. Ellis not been there I would probably never have met him. But she introduced us, and to my relief and pleasure I discovered as gentle, generous and welcoming a person as I have met, in Campden or elsewhere. I asked him then if I might come over and record him, and without hesitating he said yes. After several visits he showed me some writing he had been doing in a notebook: the first pages of his memories of Campden, which he had started for his grandchildren. I don't remember now how far into his story he had written. I do remember that by the time he reached his schooldays so many earlier memories had come up that he scrapped the whole thing and started again. Then he didn't stop. Each time I came up to record our conversations about Campden he had another twenty pages or so waiting, in the order in which they appear in this book. This book is almost how he wrote it - something discussed in a bit more detail below.

For me, the book was an ongoing revelation. Despite the volumes which have been written about Campden, nothing like it had previously been published. I asked him whether he had considered publishing it, and would he mind if it were. In fact he had been writing it only with his family and grandchildren in mind; but if one or two changes were made he would be quite happy to see it published. That was the beginning.

The changes he felt necessary had to do with a handful of remarks or memories which might embarrass or hurt certain living individuals; the changes, which are very minimal, were easily made. Other changes, which I have made, involve spelling, punctuation, the making of paragraphs, and artificially dividing the text into headed sections. In one or two instances I have inserted material into the text (as opposed to footnoting it), in which case it has been placed between square brackets, [like this]. There have been several corrections of historical detail - such as the name of a particular regiment mentioned during the course of Mr. Coldicott's reminiscences of World War II - which were suggested by members of the Historical Society Committee. There have been relatively few changes, however, and these have been with Mr. Coldicott's approval. Any mistakes which remain must really be considered my responsibility.

Mr. Coldicott completed his "Memories of an Old Campdonian" (the title he gave his notebook in 1985) about eight years ago. The adventures of the text since then - which have included quotation on television and rejection by one publisher because it was too risqué - would fill a chapter. That it is being published now is to the greatest credit of the Campden and District Historical and Archaeological Society. A century after Campden first began to be written about in earnest, the Society has had the vision to break new ground: it publishes for the first time the full reminiscence of Campden by a Campden man. I think they have reason to be proud, and I hope the reader, having shared Mr. Coldicott's world and the Campden in which he has lived, will concur.

ACKNOWLEDGEMENTS

It will be clear from the above that many thanks are due to the Committee of the Campden and District Historical and Archaeological Society for their vision, and for making the publication of this book possible. They have also given considerable practical support - many hours reading and re-reading the text, pointing out editorial mistakes and inconsistencies, suggesting possible clarifications and indicating potential footnotes. Peter Gordon, Chairman of the Society at the time the decision to publish the book was taken, has been extremely positive and supportive throughout; Felicity and Geoffrey Powell have put in a great deal of time and thought, and Felicity prepared the foundation of the Index; Allan Warmington has been a friend in need and deed, and has seen to the practical details of publication; and other members of the Committee have anonymously offered their notes and insights.

The photographs of Chipping Campden Market Hall on page iv and of Jim "Teapot" Williams on page 52d are by Roland Dyer, and are published here with the kind permission of the Guild of Handicraft Trust and Mrs. Rosemary Chapman.

The Evesham Journal (The Journal Series) have kindly given their permission to use the photograph of Mr. Coldicott which appears on the back cover.

I would also like to thank my wife, Fiona, for tireless proofreading. She and Mr. Coldicott's wife Nancy, must also be thanked for their patience and support, which have made the book possible.

SOURCES FOR FOOTNOTES

There are no footnotes in Mr. Coldicott's original text. There were a number of points, however, at which members of the Historical Society Committee strongly felt there should be some additional information. I added to this, so that there are now just over a dozen footnotes. I hope these are not obtrusive; indeed, I hope the reader may find them not only helpful, but genuinely interesting. To keep the clutter in Mr. Coldicott's text to a minimum, and where the footnote itself is not self-explanatory, the source for the footnote is given below.

p. 5; The Tithe Barn: Evesham Journal 20.9.1919,7.

p. 7; "Butcher Jack": Mr. Coldicott, recorded interview, 10.3.1994.

p. 9; Philip Lewis: Evesham Journal 3.7.1909,11; 2.10.1926,7.

p. 13; Josephine Griffiths: Evesham Journal 31.12.1949, 2; Parish Magazine, June 1950. For Christopher Whitfield see his annotated copy of A History of Chipping Campden (1958) in the Shakespeare Birthplace Trust Record Office (Stratford-on-Avon) D 212/1.

p. 18; Volunteers: Rules of the Campden and Moreton-in-Marsh or North Cotswold Rifle Volunteer Corps, (1862) Gloucestershire Record Office Pc 1532. Evesham Journal 31.7.1880,5; 16.7.1881,5; 15.2.1908,3; 21.3.1908,7. Personal Communication from Lt. Col (Retd) H.L.T. Radice MBE, Hon. Archivist of the Gloucestershire Regiment, to Craig Fees, 20.8.1984.

p. 19; Scuttlebrook Wake: Mr. Coldicott, recorded interview, 10.3.1994.

p. 21; German Field Gun: See discussion in Craig Fees, Christmas Mumming in a North Cotswold Town: With Special Reference to Tourism, Urbanisation and Immigration-Related Social Change, (PhD. thesis, University of Leeds, 1988), Vol. 1, pages 293-298.

p. 35; Evesham Journal 8.8.1903, 6.

p. 38; Mr. Coldicott.

p. 47; Evesham Journal 10.7.1920, 7 and 8; 11.9.1920,7

p. 61; I took Graham Greene's book to Mr. Coldicott when he was in hospital. This information dates from our conversation there on 31.1.1991.

p. 62; Martha Dunn: See Fiona MacCarthy, The Simple Life, pages 85-86. There are various letters from Mrs. Dunn in the Ashbee Journals held at Kings College, Cambridge. See, for example, 14.9.1932; 7.2.1933; or 24.8.1933 where she says "...when I take 30 odd yrs off can see you so bright and jolly as when you came I thought you were a dear unsophisticated creature of moods and fancies never caring a toss for the old tabbies around all of whom I rejoiced in seeing shocked because of their hypocrisy...something young and alive was here to rouse them up - they had never had any young days poor things how I pitied them - laughed to see the fun."

p. 75; Colonel Geoffrey Powell.

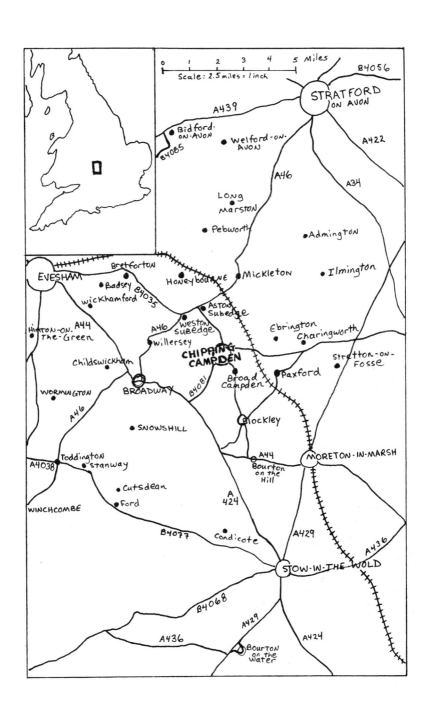

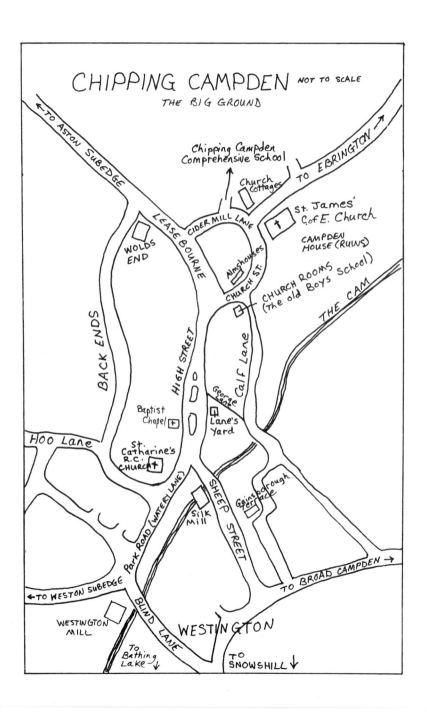

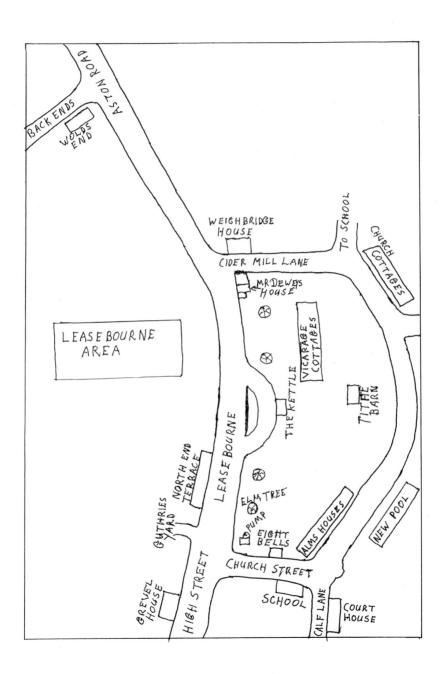

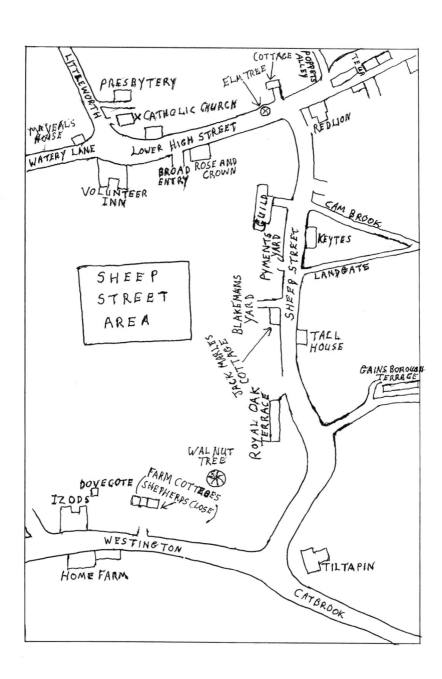

SHEEP
STREET
AREA

"My Father, and Mother, with my Grandmother Izod, in the doorway of
Grandfather Izod's Dairy in the High Street. 1903"

MEMORIES OF AN OLD CAMPDONIAN
F. W. Coldicott

1. Birth to the End of World War I

Now I am in my 76th year and have more leisure time, I thought it would be a good idea to write down some of the things that have happened during my life, and also to give my grandchildren and their generation some idea of the way of life when I was young.

I was born on Michaelmas Day, September 29th, 1910, in the house facing the Square next door to what was the Infant School, but is now the Public Library. My brother, Wilfred George, who was six years older than me, was born on January 26th, 1904, at the house next to the Police Station, in what is now the Bantam Tea Rooms. This was where my mother's father and mother lived and kept their dairy.

All my life I have always regretted the fact that I never knew either of my grandparents. They were all from well-known and old-established farming families. Grandfather Coldicott's wife was Julia Baldwyn from Ashton-under-Hill, and Grandfather Izod's wife was Elisabeth Carter from Childswickham.

Mother had another son born after me; he was christened John, but unfortunately he lived only a few weeks; he probably died from what is known as "cot death".

Both Mother and Father were quite tall and well-developed, which they should be because the Izods and the Coldicotts were all large in stature. Father was very well-liked and popular in Campden. Most people referred to him as "Canadian Jack" due to the fact, I suppose, that as a young man he spent a few years in Canada. He was christened John Rimell Coldicott but everyone, including Mother, called him "Jack". It was the same with Mother; she was christened Ellen but was always known as "Nellie".

I had a very happy childhood: in fact we were a happy, contented, and close family. Looking back now I would say that my Father's only fault was he was too happy-go-lucky, if you can really call that a fault. Winter evenings I remember there was always a jolly good fire, and after Mother had lighted the paraffin lamp, we would play cards, ludo, snakes and ladders, occasionally a sing-song. If my brother happened to be out, and Mother was busy sewing or darning, Father used to get me to read him poetry or any historical stories.

1

Many times I have heard Mother say "our Fred was such a good little boy, I would sit him in his tall baby chair in the bay window, give him a tin plate and a wooden spoon, and he wouldn't be a bit of trouble." But it was a different story after I went to school. She used to say then "He's the despair of my life, I turn him out spick and span, and he comes back home like a little ragamuffin." She reckoned if there was some mud a mile away, I would find it.

My earliest memory, and it is still quite clear to me, was sitting in the window watching the Volunteers parade in the Market Square and marching off behind the Band to go to the Station at the start of the 1914 War.

When I was about four and a half years old, I suddenly disappeared. After Mother had asked the neighbours if they had seen me, naturally she started to panic. Then a knock came on the street door. When Mother answered it, there was dear old Miss Warner from the Infants School. She said "Your little boy has wandered into school, he seems to be quite happy with us, and we would love him to stay," so that was the start of my school career. Miss Warner was such a nice lady, all the children loved her, but the headmistress, a widow named Mrs. Baum, was quite a different type. Very strict, and not a very good sense of humour.

The very first neighbour I can remember living in the house next door was Police Sergeant Fry and his wife. They had no children of their own, but made quite a fuss of me. I can remember once he pretended to put some handcuffs on me. I knew he was only playing. He took me up to the Police Station, and showed me the cells where they detained people. Then, of course, I had a few mint humbugs, which he always gave me every week. Unfortunately, Sergeant Fry was transferred to Gloucester soon after, which was a sad blow to me.

Between the house where Sergeant Fry lived and Mr. Millet's bicycle shop was a passage leading to the backs of our two houses, and then carried on down to a row of cottages: This was known as Lane's Yard. The first two cottages were occupied by Bert Bruce and his family. The oldest three children were actually named "Wilkes", Mrs. Bruce's maiden name: they were Lil, Alf and Bert. Jack, Frank, Nancy and Wilfred were Bruces. Mrs. Bruce's old mother, Mrs. Wilkes, also lived with them. They were very small cottages, so it must have made the sleeping arrangements very difficult.

The middle cottage was occupied by Matthew Williams. He was an old man with a club foot, and some years previously had been landlord

2

of the Angel Inn at Broad Campden. He was a miserable old so-and-so: I think he hated all children. On market days, which took place on the last Wednesday of each month, he would often be brought home on a wheelbarrow, too drunk to stand up.

In the other two cottages lived Bert James and his wife with their three children, Charlie, Florrie and Ted. Now, Mr. James was just the opposite to Matt Williams. He was the most amiable of men; I doubt if he ever said a cross word to anyone.

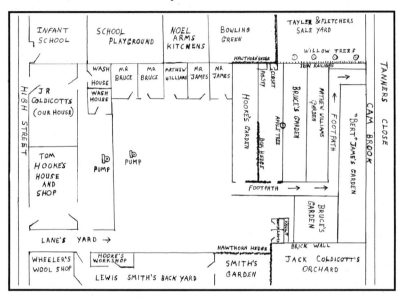

"Old Flo", as Mrs. James was known, was bred and born a real Cockney. I think originally she had come from a very respectable family, her parents kept an inn in one of the best parts of London. Unfortunately, she had taken to drink and had neglected herself, and now she looked like a character out of Dickens, with her long skirts almost dragging the floor, and only an old pair of pumps on instead of shoes. Every morning, as soon as the pubs were open, she would go down to the Red Lion, have a pint of beer at the jug and bottle lid-hole, then bring a couple of bottles back home. Towards the end of the week when her money had run out she would come and borrow money from Mother, but she never failed to return it on the Saturday. I don't think she ever did any housework, because her door was always open, and you

3

could see her sat in front of the fire, sometimes smoking an old clay pipe. Occasionally she would come and ask Mother if she could "play a tune" on the piano, and she would sit and play all the old Music Hall tunes from memory.

Our lavatories, and those of the cottages, were the old-fashioned vault type, and they were quite 120 yards away from the houses. Every household had a slop-bucket: it was a very tall galvanised bucket, with a lid, and if "nature called" during the night you had to use that. The "bogs", the usual name for the "lavs", had a wooden seat with two holes, the larger one for the grown-ups, the smaller one for the children. Somewhere near to the "bogs" were the "miskins" - they were dumps where the ashes from the fireplace and other household rubbish was kept. When the vaults were full, the husbands would team up together, form a circle with the ashes from the miskins, then take the top off the vaults and ladle the "contents" out into the circle of ashes. Then, with shovels, it was all mixed up together and spread on the various gardens. The ladles were called "gorms" - galvanised bowls with about seven or eight feet long handles. This "operation" was always done if possible on a moonlight night, with the aid of lanterns.

The gardens were quite large, and extended right down to the brook (River Cam). When I was about eight years old, Father gave me a small plot of garden about five feet square and said "There you are; that is yours." In those days you could buy two penny packets of seeds in Elsley's shop, and I used to grow lettuce, beetroot, turnips, onions, etc., and always felt so proud to take the results to Mother. Of course, she always said they were the very best.

On our garden Father had a pig-sty, and Mother a poultry run. She loved her hens, and made quite a bit of "pin" money selling eggs. Father always kept two pigs, one to sell and one for the House. Us lads used to get so attached to them, and always shed a few tears when old Ted Ladbrook came to kill them. It was a busy time when a pig was killed. There were the chitterlings to be thoroughly cleaned and salted, lard to be made from the leaf, etc., faggots to be made, at least half a dozen pork pies, and the head etc. to be boiled, and made into collared head, or what is known now as brawn. In the pantry was a large salting trough, where Father cured the flitches and hams. Women were never allowed to touch any of this during the curing period. When the curing was completed, the flitches and hams were hung on a wall in the kitchen: Father used to say "Those are the sort of pictures to have". Another saying of his was "You can use everything of a pig, except the squeal".

On these occasions all the neighbours would bring a dinner plate, and

4

Mother would give each one something: a pork pie, some faggots, or pig's liver, whichever they preferred.

In those days there was a thriving Pig Club in Campden. Each member paid one shilling per month for each pig they kept; the committee had the right to inspect your pigs at any time; if a pig died, they would pay you the value. They bought pig meal in bulk, and sold it to the members at a cheaper rate. They used the Tithe Barn* for a storage place.

Father's sister, Mrs. George Haines, owned Elmfield House, where the Catholic nuns now reside. At the rear was an orchard with access to Back Ends. Father had the use of this, where he kept a couple of breeding sows and poultry. When I was old enough I used to go and shut up the poultry every evening.

Sometimes I used to help my brother to take a sow down to Haydon's Mill, where they kept a boar. Old Noah Bennett the miller, who looked after the boar, used to say: "Now, you count how many times the boar blinks, because every time he blinks, that's a little pig."

We always hated going to have our hair cut. Father would never allow our hair to become untidy, so it meant we had to go to old Jack Marles's cottage at the bottom of Blakeman's Yard in Sheep Street for a haircut. Jack Marles, who lived on his own, was badly handicapped with a crippled leg, and could only walk with the aid of a crutch. He used to cut our hair off as close to the head as possible, except for a small fringe in the front, and if you moved he was liable to cuff you around the ear. He was a grumpy old so-and-so, and as you can imagine, we were glad to give him the two pence and get away. There was a barber's shop in Campden kept by Beckett's, but I think Father sent us to old Marles because he was glad of the coppers. Jimmy "Teapot" Williams and Charlie Hibberd were both also badly crippled, but had to work hard to keep themselves. There were no benefits of any sort in those days.

Although Campden had its own gas company, it was only used for lighting purposes, so all the working class houses only had a small oven attached to the fireplace for cooking. This created problems, especially at Christmas time, when every family had a much larger joint of meat, or a goose, turkey, etc. Tommy Heritage, who kept the bakery in the Lower

* *The Tithe Barn, adjacent to the Vicarage and opposite the parish church, was sold with its yard to a Moreton-in-Marsh solicitor in 1919 for £450. It was torn down between the wars, and the present Tithe House built on the site for Campden historian/author Christopher Whitfield.*

5

High Street where Gabb's are now,* always had his ovens in action on Christmas morning, and people could take their joint or whatever to be cooked. Then, when it was time for your meal, you could go along and fetch it straight out of the oven. Whatever you sent, the charge was sixpence, and it was always cooked lovely. In those days geese were very popular, because it was considered that goose grease was a wonderful cure for any chest complaint, such as pneumonia, etc.

I can remember when I was about six years old, there was a travelling picture show came for a week into Garnet Keyte's coal-yard in Sheep Street. I'm afraid I don't remember much about the pictures, but I can always remember they had a comedian on at half-time - he was called "Seaweed", and he sang a comic song called "Henry the Eighth I am, I am".

Father was too old for the Forces, so during the early part of the 1914-18 War he helped as a postman and fireman. He was what they called an "auxiliary postman"; he never had a uniform, just an arm-band.

Down the side of the footpath at the rear of our houses was a long, thick box-hedge. This was a very popular place for snails, and every so often some of the Ellis family would come round and collect them in a bucket. The Ellis' place was between the two butchers' shops - Smith's and Coldicott's. Harry Ellis, the father, kept the basket-making place at the rear, and Mrs. Ellis (his second wife) had her shop in the front. She kept a fish, game and poultry business, also crockery-ware, etc. She was an old "dragon", and us kids were a bit scared of her, but when I was older I found her very useful, because I could always sell her a few pheasants.

Every year without fail one or two circuses came to Campden, usually in Badger's Field (where the old people's homes are now). They were always sure of a full house. People patronised them because there were no home entertainments like television, radio, or even gramophones.

I remember my brother and I used to visit and play with Joseph and Frank Jones. Joe was about my brother's age, and Frank was my age. They lived up an alley next to the Kettle in Leaseborne, and their parents had a Polyphone. It played a large metal disc, like a circular saw; we thought it was wonderful. In the cottage opposite to them in the passage lived old Minnie Nichols, who used to make lovely long twisted

* *Now, in 1994, this is the pet shop called Creature Comforts, run by Joy Gabb.*

6

sticks of treacle rock. They were a half-penny each. We did enjoy them. Sometimes she would let us go in and watch her making them.

Dad's brother, Uncle Bob, and Aunty Lil his wife lived at the Kettle. Before her marriage she was Lillian Evans from Blockley; her father had the piano factory there. Aunty Lil kept the grocery and provisions shop, and Uncle Bob was a fruit and vegetable merchant. He had the orchard at Catbrook where Cherry Orchard Close is now; four acres in the Big Ground, behind what is now Coneygree Close; and two fields on the left of the road the other side of the railway bridge.

Father had three acres next to Uncle Bob's in the Big Ground, and another two acres in the Oddfellows'; this was land owned by the Oddfellows Benefit Society, who let it out to rent. Today it is the Berrington Road Council Estate.

I remember we had an acre of wheat in the Big Ground. One morning Father came hurrying back home. He had seen a deer in the corn: he grabbed his twelve bore gun, and dashed back again. He shot the deer, and brought it home on Uncle Bob's dray - there was no need to go to the butcher for a while. That is the only time I have ever had venison. In those days there was a herd of deer in Northwick Park; it must have escaped from there.

Father was always considered to be a first class shot. I have seen him pick off the first and last birds of a covey of partridges several times. Jack Coldicott, the butcher*; Tom Hopkins, another butcher; Norman Izod, Sam Gladwin, and my Father formed a syndicate, and for years had the shooting rights on several farms, including Weston Park. They usually went every Thursday, because that was early closing day for the shops.

In 1916 Campden had the worst snow ever. I can remember Father carrying me on his shoulder near the Churchyard, to see them digging a way through to get to Campden Station. Everyone who could use a shovel was helping, including the schools.

The mails from the Post Office had to be taken to the Station every

---

*No relation to Mr. Coldicott's father, also 'Jack'. No one in Campden got them confused: "Father was always called Canadian Jack, and the other was called Butcher Jack, and that's how they distinguished them. Nobody ever referred to Dad as Jack, they'd always say 'Old Canadian' or 'Old Butcher Jack'. They were good pals. They were a right pair, I think, to be honest. Butcher Jack was a bit of a relation to the Haines through his mother, I think, but not to the Coldicott side."

evening and put on the mail train. The Noel Arms had the contract to take them in their horse-drawn coach. Ben Benfield was the hostler. One evening his nephew went with him for a ride; he rode inside the coach with the mail. On the journey he opened the mail bags, took out the registered letters, and tied the bags up again. The police found the empty envelopes, and the nephew confessed. At Gloucester Assizes he was sent down for six months. He never returned to Campden, but settled down in Bristol.

About this time Father's oldest brother, Uncle William Coldicott, died at Broad Campden. He was a huge man, six feet four inches, and weighed twenty-two stones. He married Alice Griffin, daughter of the landlord of the Volunteer Inn; they never had any children. As I remember him he was crippled up with rheumatism. His wife had been dead some years, and he had a house keeper named Mrs. Smith, a farmer's daughter from Winchcombe. She used to make quite a fuss of me and my brother.

I find it very difficult to understand why everyone seems to make the excuse these days that the youngsters are bored. We had no radios or televisions, but my word, we were never bored; the days didn't seem long enough for us. As long as the light nights permitted we practically lived down in the fields and in the brook. "Follow the leader" was one of our favourite games. Whatever the leader did, the others had to do the same; the object was to try and do something the others daren't do. I remember once when I was leader, I climbed a tree in the Calfs House Ground, and jumped out into the field. When I landed my knee struck my chin, and for about half a minute I was completely knocked out.

Practically every boy had an iron hoop (girls had wooden ones). Our favourite hooping run was down Calfs Lane. Now it is hardly safe to walk down there. Sometimes we would have a session with our whips and tops, up and down the street, or play marbles up the gutters at the side of the pavements. Of course it would be impossible to play any games on the highway now-a-days. The girls' most popular game was hopscotch on the pavement. When it was wet we would gather in the old Market Hall, and play either tig, or tig-tag-toe, otherwise known as "five stones": Each player had three small pebbles, or flat stones. One player had one pebble, put his hands behind his back, and his opponent had to try to guess which hand held the pebble. If he chose the hand with the pebble in, he would shout "tig-tag-toe my first go." The game was the first one to get three pebbles in a direct line.

8

Campden always had a good football team. The first pitch I can remember was at Court Piece, then they moved to the opposite side of Dyers Lane into the Leasow. From there they moved to Loveridge where they stayed until the Recreation Ground was opened in 1928.

One of Father's friends was Mr. Geoffrey Smith at Attlepin Farm, and I remember me and my brother were there, it must have been during the summer holidays. Anyway, one of the cart horses had got a foal, so Bill (my brother hated the name "Wilfred") said, "I wonder what mare's milk tastes like?" He asked the servant girl, Rose Fisher from Weston Sub-Edge, for a clean tin. I held the tin whilst Bill milked the mare. She didn't mind a bit. We each had a drink, and as far as I can remember, it tasted quite sweet.

When Mr. Smith retired, they lived at "Hollybush", Broad Campden. There his wife had a narrow escape. She was sat at the table one day, when without warning the blue stone floor under the table caved in, revealing a very deep well, with quite a depth of water in it.

When I was about eight years old I started going over to the Baptist Chapel to Sunday School. It was held in a large room behind the chapel. There were quite a lot of children of other denominations used to attend. They never tried to convert us, or overdo the religious side. Of course we always sang a couple of hymns, and a prayer at the start and finish. We always enjoyed the talks on foreign countries, and the indoor games. There was quite a large collection of books, which you were allowed to take home and read. All three of the ladies who took Sunday School were spinsters: they were Miss How from Westington, Lil Court (her father was "Happy Joe" Court who was caretaker), and Jane Badham, the eldest of the three. She was a sister to "Echo" Badham, who occasionally preached in Chapel. They were three very patient and tolerant women; they had to be, with some of us little heathens.

The Reverend "Pa" Lewis was still active at the Chapel, but he didn't live at the Manse then. He lived at Catbrook, in one of the houses the Guild of Handicraft built. He was a dapper little Welshman, very dogmatic, and no sense of humour.*

When I was seven years old I had to leave the Infants School for the

* *The Rev. Philip Lewis: Campden's Baptist minister from 1885 to 1892. Returned by popular demand in 1895, retired in 1909, died at Catbrook in 1926 aged 89. From the moment he stepped foot in Campden he breathed tangible vitality into the Baptist congregation, courting controversy and taking the lead in Radical (Liberal) politics. He found welcome allies in Ashbee, Alec Miller and other members of the Guild.*

Boys School, opposite the Eight Bells, now used as the Church Rooms. The headmaster was Mr. George Dewey, and his assistant was Miss "Pat" Lavendar. Mr. Dewey's wife was headmistress of the Girls School, known as the Blue School, in the High Street next to Grevel House. Although a well educated man, he was quite unfit to be a headmaster. He really was a sadist, couldn't control his temper, and I'm sure enjoyed doling out punishment. He was always calling us "Campden Pigs, only fit to follow the plough".

At the rear of Coldicott's Butcher Shop was an orchard. This ran parallel to our gardens, with about a five foot high wall between. Of course us kids used to nip over and nick a few apples occasionally, but on one occasion we were really caught napping. There was Bill, myself, Charlie James, Alf Wilkes ("Oily"), Bert Wilkes, and Ernie Hayden, one of blacksmith Hayden's boys. When we were safely back over with our pockets filled, out from behind the loos came Butcher Jack with a thin stick. He'd seen us in his orchard, popped along the street, and down our back yard. Needless to say, we ran in all directions. Bill and "Oily" Wilkes dived into the loos, let their trousers down pretending to answer the call of Nature, but it didn't work, they each had a couple on their bare buttocks. I had jumped over into our pig-sty; old Jack came and looked over the door at the two pigs. I was crouched in a corner of the pen with my heart thumping, and luckily I got away with it. A couple of the others had a swipe on their backsides as they ran up the path. As far as I can remember, that was our last raid over the wall.

I well remember one day during the holidays, me, Charlie James, Bert Wilkes and Jack Bruce were playing hopscotch on the blue bricks outside the Armoury (now the Midland Bank), when George ("Lucas") Greenall came, and said "there is a table at the entrance to the chemist's shop full of small bars of chocolate, it would be quite easy to take some." Off we all went up the street. When we thought the coast was clear, we each grabbed some chocolate, and walked away to go up Church Street. Reg Hands, who owned the chemist's, must have spotted us. He came dashing round the corner, and off we all ran. As we turned the corner into Calfs Lane he wasn't far behind us. Coming up Calfs Lane were Harry Griffin and "Wacky" Holtom, two road men. Reg Hands shouted to them to stop us. They took us back to the chemist's, and locked us in a greenhouse behind the shop, and told us "there you will stay until your parents come for you."

Eventually, George Greenall's mother came, and then my father and Mrs. Bruce turned up, and rather than leave poor little Charlie James on his own, Reg Hands let him go with Mrs. Bruce. The oldest of us,

"Lucas" Greenall, was only nine years old, so I suppose the police were not told because of our ages. Only twice did Father ever hit me, and this was the first. He gave me a few across my backside. The second time was when he caught me and Alf Wilkes sucking eggs in Mother's hen roost. He gave me and "Oily" a good slap on the backside with his belt.

On the last Wednesday of every month there was a stock sale. The sheep were on sale in the Square, in pens formed with hurdles. The cattle and pigs were in pens at the rear of the Noel Arms. Hutchings and Deer from Stratford-on-Avon were the auctioneers - later on it was taken over by Tayler and Fletcher from Stow-on-the-Wold. When they held the Prize Teg Show Sales, the sheep pens stretched up the street nearly as far as the Lygon Arms. The hurdles forming the pens were always erected by three old Campden characters. They were Joey Quinn, George "Ninety" Griffin, and Jimmy "Teapot" Williams. Sometimes, if it was a large sale, Dick "Corporal" Keen, who had spent all his life in the army, would help out. After the sale they had to stack away all the hurdles at the rear of the Noel Arms, and swill down the Square, etc.

We always welcomed the sale days, it gave us the opportunity to earn a few coppers. The majority of the livestock was bought for Birmingham butchers, and had to be transported by the Great Western Railway, so they were glad of us boys to drive the cattle, sheep and pigs to the station, and load them in the trucks. There were a few regular drovers, like Charlie Seitz (known as "Sykes"). He was an Anglo-Indian, born in Bombay, the son of a wealthy Indian doctor. He had been a student assistant to Doctor Morris at Cotswold House, and won a diploma from the Royal College of Surgeons. Unfortunately his brain "snapped", and he finished up as a cattle drover. He was a very fearsome-looking man, but quite harmless. I never knew him to be nasty to anyone, except once in Stratford-on-Avon the police tried to arrest him for being intoxicated, and it took quite a number of them to overpower him. He had escaped three times.

One of the loveliest features of the countryside is now practically extinct: that is the cherry orchards. When I was a lad, there were five large orchards and two smaller ones in Campden and Broad Campden. At Broad Campden they were at Briar Hill Farm, and W.N. Izod's, at the rear of his farmhouse. At Campden there was Hand's Orchard, opposite side of the road to the Coneygree; George Haines' at Westington, and Attlepin Farm; then there was a smaller one in Gainsborough's, behind the old Ruins, and Uncle Bob's at Catbrook. Now every year there is the "Plum Run" around the Vale of Evesham, when the plum trees are in blossom, but it does not compare with the lovely cherry blossom. It was

11

magnificent, there were always several sorts of cherry in each orchard, and each had a slightly different tint.

Every orchard had to have a bird-minder for five or six weeks. This was usually someone who was not quite able-bodied enough to do regular work. "Teapot" Williams, who was a cripple, was always on duty at Hand's Orchard in Station Road. It meant being there from dawn to dark. They were provided with a gun and rattle. The cherry-picking season was always a boon to casual workers; for a few weeks they could earn good money: the more they picked, the more they earned.

When unions and government laid down a wages policy it was just impossible to employ cherry-minders; it would have meant paying them over £200 a week, because the law said that anything over the forty hour week would be classed as overtime, and of course it was essential to be there all the hours of daylight. Thus the decline of cherry orchards.

During the Great War the Boys School spent one half day a week blackberry picking during the season. When we got them back to school they were put into small tubs, which held about forty pounds, then they were taken to the Station, where they were transported to a jam factory and made into jam for the troops abroad.

For quite a number of years after the war I went blackberrying after school and week-ends; some of the women in Campden accumulated quite a nice sum of money every year. Weston Park was a favourite place to go -- one part in particular, locally known as "Beachey Bank". There were always masses of quite large blackberries there, and you could always call in at Mr. George Vinn's in Watery Lane and sell them. The usual price was around penny three farthings, or two pence, a pound. "Happy" Joe Court also bought blackberries, so really it was a case of finding out who was paying the best price.

"Happy" Joe Court lived opposite the Roman Catholic Church. He was a real old Campden character. He was the father of Lil Court, who, as I mentioned before, was one of the teachers at the Baptist Sunday School. For years Joe was caretaker at the chapel, and he also was organ blower: he had to sit behind the organ, pumping a long lever up and down. After the Noel Arms gave up taking the mail to Campden Station, Joe took the job on. He also collected the household rubbish with his horse and dray; the rubbish tip then was at Horseman's Corner, half-way between Westington and the Cross Hands. Joe had always got a smile on his face, and a cheery word for everybody. He wore the same battered old bowler hat weekdays and Sundays.

Quite a few of the old timers wore the black bowler hats. Charlie

12

"Slap" Blakeman was one. Now, "Slap" was indeed a character. By profession he was a horse breaker, and Doctor Dewhurst reckoned he must have broken nearly every bone in his body, and that his skull was twice as thick as an ordinary man's.

Slap lived at Westington in one of the cottages at the end of the lane next to Gladwin's farm (now turned into one large house). The best way to describe him would be to say he was a crafty, drunken old twister. During his life, he must have had over thirty convictions for being drunk and disorderly. Although he had a bad stutter in his speech, he always had a quick answer for everything. The stories of his crafty tricks, especially about the buying and selling of horses, would fill another book.

One story of his craftiness I must record. It is perfectly true. On one occasion he had broken a leg, and had borrowed a three-wheeled invalid chair from the Vicarage. There was a poor young man in Campden then named Bob Minchin, who was quite badly mentally retarded. Slap got Bob to push him around in this old basket chair, with an old horse blanket over him to keep him warm. Under the blanket he kept a quart bottle to piddle in. Bob had pushed him to the Volunteer Inn, where Slap had some drink. Then he got Bob to take him around Back Ends to see if his horse was alright in a field there. When they got to the bank at Wold's End, Bob loosed the handle, and down the bank went Slap on his own. At the junction with Aston Road, over went the chair tipping Slap out and breaking his bottle. Dear old Miss Griffiths, who was walking down Aston Road at the time, ran up to Slap saying, "Oh dear, Mr. Blakeman, what have you done, are you hurt?" "No ma'am," says Slap, "I think I shall be alright, but it has broken my bottle of whiskey." "Oh, what a shame; here is some money to buy yourself another one," said Miss Griffiths* .

I well remember one day, when I came home from school at mid-day, Mother said, "the dinner isn't quite ready, I want you to pop up to the

---

* *Josephine Griffiths (1865-1949): "a wit, a saint, and a scholar", "...for her Campden, its church and its people, was life itself." Quiet benefactor, much-loved member of the established Griffiths family of Bedfont House. A natural but self-effacing local historian (her book "Chipping Campden, Today and Yesterday", was published anonymously in 1931) who gathered together and freely shared Campden history and memories, for example with Christopher Whitfield for his "History of Chipping Campden". Left a loving body of manuscript material including the "Book of Remembrance" in the Church, in which she recorded details of the lives of local men killed in the 1914-18 War.*

chemist's for me before they close at one o'clock." When I came out of the shop, without any warning old Slap gave me such a clout across the back with his walking stick, and I said, "I didn't call after you Mr. Blakeman." He stuttered and said, "N-n-no, that's for when you b-bloody well do." I was about nine or ten years old at the time.

Another old character was George "Beefbone" Smith, who lived with his old sister Sarah in one of Hull's Cottages at Broad Campden. About twice a week he would walk over to Campden, coming down George Lane, and up through the Noel Arms. Albert Tanner was the landlord at the Noel Arms, and whenever they met each other, they would stand and shout at each other, using the most vile language and insulting each other. When Beefbone died, Sarah, his sister, didn't live very long after. When they went "to lay her out", they couldn't take her stays off, the flesh had actually grown over the metal ribs.

As I drive around the country roads these days, my thoughts go back to the old Council roadmen. In my opinion the state of the roads has deteriorated, excluding the main roads. In every village or small town there were several local roadmen. In Campden when I was a lad I can well remember there was old Bill Hughes with his tricycle, "Wacky" Holtom, Harry Griffin, and little Billy Cherry. Each had their own section, and took pride in keeping it clean and tidy: the sides were always trimmed and the storm gouts shovelled out. Old Bill Hughes's section was along the main road from the Cross Hands to the top of Broadway Hill; he used to travel up there on his tricycle until he was over seventy years of age.

Wacky Holtom was a nasty-tempered, cantankerous man. The saying was that one day a gentleman asked him where the road went to. Wacky said "It don't go anywhere, it stays where it is." The gentleman said, "Don't be a damned fool, man." Wacky said, "If there is a fool, it is you. I know where I am, but you are lost."

I am quite convinced that the winters were much more severe when I was a lad than they are now. Practically every year the ponds were frozen over thick enough to slide on, and I can remember people going over to Northwick Park to skate on the lake there. One year we were sliding on the New Pool, opposite the Almshouses, when Lewis Wheatcroft fell and broke his leg. His older brother, George, was there and carried him home to their house, right at the far end of Watery Lane. They lived there with George Vinn, who was their mother's father. They were all Plymouth Brethren, a very strict religion; they would not have a newspaper in the house, and if there were any parades, fêtes, Scuttlebrook Wake, or any functions, the children were not allowed out.

14

I used to enjoy going sledging. Down Conduit Hill was the favourite place; you could go from the little stone water house right down to Tiltapin Corner.

There was a man lived at Seymour House, a Mister Welsh. We all called him "Yabu". He had a lovely large sledge that we used to borrow; six of us could get on it at once. This Mr. Welsh was a huge man with a beard. He had travelled the world quite a bit as an explorer. Out at the back of the house he had a large stuffed alligator. When "Yabu" Welsh left Seymour House, it was sold and turned into a boarding house for the girls at the Grammar School.

I shall always remember the first time I ever fired a gun. I think I was about nine years old at the time. My brother had got Father's double-barrelled twelve bore, minding the strawberries in the Big Ground. I badly wanted to fire it, but was not quite strong enough to hold it steady when I had it to my shoulder. Anyway, Bill stuck an old bucket on a stick, and I balanced the barrels in the fork of a small apple tree. When I pulled the trigger I shut both eyes and nearly sat on my bottom, but I had peppered the old bucket. Of course, Bill was nearly crying with laughter, and when he told Father he also had a good laugh.

Towards the end of the war Dudley Haydon had a young man working for him to help get the harvest in. His name was Frank Willoughby Harris, who lived in Cider Mill Lane, next to Bob Dickinson and his wife. Willoughby was really "a penny short of a shilling", the common term for being a little mentally retarded. One day Mr. Haydon said something to Willoughby, he took offence, said "B----r your corn, I'll go and join the army". Off he went and did just that. About three months later there was a warrant out for Willoughby, he had deserted the Army. One evening old Mother Dickinson heard Willoughby's voice next door, and immediately rushed off and informed the police. The police came up and they knocked at the door. Willoughby dashed up the stairs and jumped out of the back window. There was no way out at the back, so he had to come through a passage into Cider Mill Lane. On seeing him, the two policemen ran after him, but the further they went, the further Willoughby got in front, and eventually made good his escape. About two years later Willoughby was discharged from the Army, came back to Campden, and got a regular job with Dudley Haydon.

In May 1917 one of our playmates, Harold Hayden, one of the sons of Tom Hayden, was taken ill. He had to be taken to Stratford-on-Avon in a horse and trap, but sadly, poor Harold died. At his funeral the coffin was carried by six of his pals: Joe Jones, Cecil Becket, Jim Keeley, Charlie Grove, and my brother Bill. I am not quite sure, now, but I think

15

he was 10 years old.

The school attendance officer was a man named Davis, who lived at Stow-on-the-Wold. Every week he came and inspected the school registers - if any boy had missed a day, he was very soon at the house wanting to know why. I well remember one time, it was a Campden Sale day, he knocked at our door, and when Mother came, he said, "Why isn't your lad at school?" Mother said very indignantly, "But of course he is at school." Old Davis said, "That's funny, I have just seen him sat on the sheep pens." As you may guess, I was in trouble when I went in home at tea-time.

It was in 1917 that Davis the school inspector took six parents to court for keeping a child away from school. They were the following: Ellen Howell from Broad Campden, for Alfred Wadley aged 11 years; Thomas Grove, Church Cottages, for Charles Grove aged 12 years; James Keeley, Lower High Street, for James Keeley aged 12 years; Tom Nobes, Silk Mills Yard, for Frederick Nobes aged 9 years; Tom Cross, Lower High Street, for Albert Cross aged 12 years; John Coldicott, the Square, for my brother Bill aged 12 years. They were all fined ten shillings. Tom Nobes told the magistrates he had two sons out in France, and Davis should be out there with them. All these boys had been kept away for two or three days to pick up potatoes.

About this time there was a travelling theatre came to the Town Hall for a week; it was called Fred Beebee's Travelling Players. Two of the ladies came by train, and came up from the Station in the horse bus. When the bus got to Wixey's grocery shop in Church Street, Ben Benfield, the driver, stopped to deliver a parcel in the shop, which he had done on very many occasions. This time something startled the horse, and he galloped away down the High Street. The two ladies, scared to death, were screaming for help. It could have been a very serious accident, but Frank Bennett very bravely ran into the road and managed to grab the reins, and hung on until the horse stopped.

In January of 1918 Tom Smith, who was the town crier and also caretaker of the Town Hall, accidentally fell down the stairway in the Town Hall and broke his neck. He was the grandfather of Robert Smith, the butcher. He left his widow, five sons, and six daughters.

There was a terrible epidemic of Asian flu swept through the country in 1918, definitely the worst flu epidemic that has ever been known. In Campden there were three or four funerals every week; practically every household suffered. I know we were all in bed with it at home, and Mother's brother Uncle Charlie, who was living at Miss Sansome's at

Weston Park Farm at the time, used to come down and do what he could for us each day. Thank God we all survived, but poor Uncle Charlie caught it and died.

In November 1918 the war ended, and the Armistice was signed on November 11th. There was great jubilation throughout the country, the schools had a holiday, and there was an ox roast in the Square outside the Armoury, all the local butchers helping financially and with the roasting of the ox.

"Putting in new drains at Burnt Norton for the Earl of Harrowby. 1928. Contractor, 'Bummer' Haines."

Top row, left to right: Charlie "Ganty" Bennett, Walter Matthews, George "Bungy" Dyde, Harry Taylor, Fred Coldicott, Harry Nobes, Bill Jeffries, "Bummer" Haines, Sam Byrd.
Lower row, left to right: Bert Cook, Harold Haines, Jim Harper.

2. Between the Wars

During the Great War, and for a time after the Armistice, there was obviously a great shortage of manpower, and the market gardeners in the Vale of Evesham had to rely on German prisoners of war for their labour. Joseph Webb of Mickleton was a very large grower who had a farm near the top of Broadway Hill, as well as his land and greenhouses at Mickleton. I can well remember seeing the German prisoners coming through Campden on horse-drawn drays: they were in grey clothes, with a round blue patch, about the size of a football, sewn on their backs.

After the war the local Volunteers* were re-formed and a regular army sergeant by the name of Travell was stationed here. He married a local girl named Edith Mary Plested, but in 1920 he was charged with committing bigamy. She eventually married again, and went to live in Chipping Norton, where she and her husband kept a public house. She had a brother, Ormonde Plested, who spent a number of years in Canada, then came back to Campden and married "Shoemaker" Keen's daughter, Nora. Ormonde was in charge of the fire brigade when I joined in about 1933.

The Volunteer shooting range was in a field at Broad Campden, half-way between the village and Rogue's Hill Farm. After a shooting practice, we used to go and dig out the lead bullets from the earth bank behind the targets.

After the war there was a large sale of surplus army horses and mules. A great friend of my Father's, Ernest Woolliams, who lived in Leaseborne in the house where Lewis Horne now lives[1], bought about four mules. He had no trouble selling them to local farmers and tradesmen.

In one of the cottages up Cider Mill Lane lived Jack Morris. He was an old Campdonian recently returned from Canada, and he was a real

---

* *The Campden detachment of the 8th Battalion Worcester Territorial Regiment. The local Volunteer company was first enrolled in 1860 as the Moreton and Campden, or North Cotswold Rifle Volunteers, 16th Gloucestershire Rifle Corps. In 1880 it became K Co., North Cotswold Rifle Volunteers, 2nd Gloucestershire Volunteer Rifles, and in the Cardwell reforms of the following year became K Co. of the 2nd Volunteer Battalion of the Gloucestershire Regiment. In the Haldane reforms of 1908 it became H Company, 5th Battalion Territorials, Gloucestershire Regiment.*

[1] *Leasbourne House. Lewis Horne died in 1991.*

"nut case". Anyway, he bought a lovely looking grey mare off Ernest Woolliams, and a dray from Bricknell's, the wheelwright at the Bakers Arms in Broad Campden. He would go to Evesham Market and buy a load of vegetables, and then hawk them around Campden and Broad Campden. On one occasion he bought a large quantity of onions; Bill Beckett, who was the local carrier between Campden and Evesham, was in the market when old Jack bought these onions. Later, when he was hawking them around Campden, Bill Beckett said, "Jack, you can't go on like that, you're selling them for less than you paid for them." Jack says, "Ah, it's alright, Mr. Beckett, it's the quantity I sells."

One time he pinned a notice on his door saying "tame rabbits wanted". I had a black and white rabbit I wanted to get rid of, so I got Jack Harris to come with me (scared to go on my own). We knocked at the door, and old Jack shouted "Come in". When we opened the door and went in, there were rabbits running about all over the floor. There was a pile of ashes in the grate. Jack went to them, running his fingers through, and says, "Look at that, boys, Gold, lovely Gold." He gave me half-a-crown for my rabbit, and we couldn't get out of that door quick enough.

At Scuttlebrook Wake* the crowd were enjoying themselves when without any warning there was pandemonium: Jack Morris came galloping through on his grey mare firing a double-barrel twelve bore gun into the air. He had a bandolier of cartridges round his waist, and a coloured blanket or rug instead of a saddle: he looked a typical bandit. Poor old Jack, after that he was certified insane, and that was the last Campden saw of him. George Hart, who was then at Attlepin Farm, bought the horse and dray.

Mr. Horace Badger, who lived in the house between the Police Station

---

* *Scuttlebrook Wake: Campden's annual Whit Saturday festival now celebrated with a travelling fair in Leaseborne (under which the "Scuttle" Brook, now enclosed, still runs), and Maypole and other dancing and festivities in the Square: "When I was a young lad there was always a boxing booth came, there were various sideshows, dancing troupes, a tent with animals with mutations, like a duck with three legs, and very often a wild west show was included. And it was a really a wonderful sight to see the old traction engines that brought these various shows here. They were lovely, they were all polished brass, and they looked lovely. And in those days it was a meeting place for the families, it really was, and you'd get families come from Ebrington, they'd come in from Weston Subedge and Blockley, and they all met the old Campden people, and they had a night out together. It was a real meeting place for families, it really was."*

and Morrey's Stores, had four fields adjoining George Lane at the rear of the Noel Arms. Over the years he had built up a first class herd of dairy cows; they were his "pride and joy". But sadly, about 1920 foot and mouth disease struck the herd; every animal on the farm had to be destroyed. A huge pit was excavated where the old peoples' homes are now, and all the bodies were dumped in and covered with lime. At the bottom of the gardens where we lived was a row of withy trees near the brook; several of us lads climbed up the trees and watched. It was heartbreaking to see those lovely cows being destroyed. Heaven knows how the Badger family felt.

My father's friend Ernest Woolliams, who was a horse and cattle dealer, had left Leaseborne in Campden and was living at Holt Farm near Blockley. About two or three years after the affair at Mr. Badger's, I well remember Mr. Woolliams on one of his visits to see Father telling him he had discovered foot and mouth disease in some of his cows, and had successfully cured them.

These old dealers never had veterinary surgeons. I remember a Miss Mostyn had a lovely cream-coloured hunter. She had the vet to it who told her nothing could be done, it would have to be put down. It was taken to Dan Perkins's knacker yard at Weston-Sub-Edge to be destroyed. A few months later Miss Mostyn recognised her horse near Evesham, and found out Dan had completely cured it and then sold it. There was some trouble over it, but it never went to law; I don't expect the vet wanted it publicised.

In June 1922 when I was twelve Horace Badger found the body of a lady I knew in Haydon's Mill Pond. She was wearing several thick skirts. We watched the police and others get her body out and take it away on Joe Court's dray. She was a sister of old Jack Morris's, and had been mentally ill for some time.

In February 1920 a captured German field gun arrived in Campden. A concrete base was prepared for it in front of the Martins near the Market Hall. On the 13th of March it was placed in position and handed over into the care of the Parish Council. You can just imagine how popular it was with all the boys, playing at soldiers.

During the night of May 24th (Empire Day), the gun was removed from its base and dumped in the middle of the New Pool. The Parish Council had it returned and put back on its base, but it was only for a short stay. It was again taken in the night. This time it was discovered in Sloshy Walker's mill pond at Berrington Mill. The Council decided there was no point in retaining it, so the Earl of Harrowby took to it, and had it removed to his house at Burnt Norton*.

At the end of March 1920, Aunt Julia's husband George Haines died, aged 75 years. He had been a good servant to Campden and surrounding district: for 37 years a member of the Shipston-on-Stour Board of Governors; chairman of Campden Rural District Council; first chairman of the Campden Parish Council; member of the Town Trust; chairman of the Flower Show Committee; and Churchwarden, etc. It was about this time, I remember, that the landlord of the George and Dragon was committed to jail for one month for attempted suicide. I think he had been drinking heavily for a time, and had cut his throat and wrists.

Campden had always been connected with the wool trade, and in July 1920, Tayler and Fletcher the auctioneers, who were running the monthly stock market, decided to revive the annual wool sale. There were 81 lots; a total of 7,000 fleeces were sold.

It was very interesting when we came down the street from school to stand and watch Edgar Keen carving the names and dates of those unfortunate men who had lost their lives during the war on the new war memorial. I often wondered what his thoughts were, because he had known them all. Edgar Keen was a local lad, son of John "Shoemaker" Keen. It was his sister, Nora, who married Ormonde Plested. He had a brother, Arthur, who was chauffeur at the Noel Arms. Edgar afterwards emigrated to America. He had learnt his sculpture and carving under Alec Miller, who came to Campden with Ashbee and the Guild of Handicraft.†

* *The German field gun affair: One in five Campden men served in the 1914-18 War. Of these one in five died. Others (such as Jack Horne, who appears in this book), returned wounded or maimed. Others slowly died from the effects of wounds and gas. The gun, offered by the War Trophies Commission, was accepted by the parish council and the Comrades of the Great War in something of the pre-War, Victorian spirit of patriotism. A group of primarily younger Campden men decided that they would not have such a "trophy", which may have killed their friends and comrades, sitting in the centre of Campden. They removed it twice, the second and final time in a festive but no-nonsense torchlight procession, reading "military orders" and singing war time songs. Similar emotions surrounded the war memorial, but here they appear to have been resolved in the creation of a major new architectural feature dedicated not to war or killing, but to the commemoration of everything Campden had lost, focussed in the 61 men whose names Edgar Keen carved.*

† *See Editor's Introduction.*

21

The war memorial was completed, and the unveiling ceremony was performed in January 1921 by Major General Reginald Stephens, K.C.B., C.M.G. It was designed by F L. Griggs.

On the 7th of May 1921 there was a property sale, where John Skey, the landlord, bought the Lygon Arms, a freehouse, for £1,140.

On June 4th, 1921, Mother's uncle, William Nathan Izod ("Big Shilling") died at Broad Campden. In 1868 he married the daughter of William Wynniatt from Buckland. He left four sons - William, Wolford, Ernest, Douglas -, and one daughter, Anne. I have never found out the reason why, but he and my grandfather, who were brothers, never spoke to each other after their father died. He left £7,456/14/1d gross estate; net personal, £5,854/16/9d. When he was a young man, he was Colour Sergeant in the Volunteers, and considered to be the best shot with a rifle in the company.

1922 was the first year we ever had a school outing. We went in a charabanc to Oxford for the day; most of us had never been any further than Evesham. The colleges at Oxford were on their summer vacation, but it had been arranged for us to be shown around Magdalen, and I shall always remember they took us down into the kitchens, where the cockroaches ran in all directions.

This was the first time we had ever seen a Woolworths store; we were spellbound, and what money we had got, we spent the lot in there. In those days everything was threepence or sixpence. I can still remember one of the things I bought was a water pistol; I had never seen one before. On the journey back to Campden we must have looked like a lot of natives with their war paint on: practically everyone had bought transfers from Woolworths. They were paper squares, about two inches by two inches, with gaudy coloured butterflies, etc., on them. You put them on your flesh, wetted the back well, and then peeled the paper off, leaving the coloured part on, looking like a tattoo. That year there was a song came out called "I'm forever blowing bubbles"; I can well remember we were all singing that on the way home.

There was no school outing the following year, but 1924, the year of the Great Exhibition at Wembley, the outing was to go there by train. We had been saving up at school for this, and then a couple of weeks before the day I asked "Boss" Dewey for the money I had saved. He was furious, but he couldn't refuse me, so I had it out and bought a second-hand bicycle from Stacey Tombs' shop in Bengeworth, Evesham. I think one of the reasons why I suddenly altered my mind about the outing to Wembley was the fact that about three weeks previously I had to hire a

22

bicycle from Mr. Badham's to go over to Blockley on the day of the funerals of the women killed in the terrible bus accident.

What happened at Blockley was, a party of local women had gone to a fête at Stanton in a bus belonging to the local garage owner, George Rouse. On the journey back home everyone was in high spirits and enjoying themselves. When they turned off the main road to come down the steep hill into the village, known as the Greenway, the bus suddenly started gathering speed. Some of the women started shouting at Dennis Sharpe, the driver, but the poor fellow was helpless, the brakes had completely failed. At the bottom of the Greenway is a T-junction, and across the road opposite the Greenway there is an eight foot high stone wall. The situation facing Dennis Sharpe was hopeless, there was nothing he could do. The bus crashed into the wall and overturned. Four of the ladies were killed outright, and four more died a few hours later from their injuries. The wall the bus crashed into actually was the garden wall of Doctor Jacob's house; fortunately, he was on the scene almost immediately.

When I went to Mr. Badham's I paid him one shilling for two hours, but when I got back from Blockley I had been away nearly four hours. I hadn't any more money, so I left the bicycle up old "Donkey" Badham's passage, and ran away.

Dennis Sharpe, the driver of the bus, broke both his wrists in the accident, but continued to drive for George Rouse for a number of years afterwards.

I can well remember the first aeroplane I ever saw on the ground, I think it was just after the Great War ended. How the news came to Campden I don't know, but we heard that a plane which was on its way to Ireland had made a forced landing in the Hundred Acre field near Weston-Sub-Edge Station. I know a crowd of us lads made our way down there as soon as we came out of school. As far as I can remember, it was a two-seater bi-plane.

Not long after that Dick Clarke landed in a single wing plane near Campden Station. He was in the Royal Flying Corps at the time. His parents lived at Battledene Farm. His father owned the factory which is now the Campden Research Station. He stayed the night with his parents, and there was a huge crowd watched him take off the following day. He was a fine looking young man, and could easily have been mistaken for the Prince of Wales.

Mr. Clarke's factory was originally built for producing pheasant feeds. There was a very large painting of a cock pheasant painted on the factory wall facing the railway line. All through the Great War it was commandeered by the government and used for making army biscuits.

One feature of country life that will never be seen again is the steam ploughing. It was a lovely sight to see those two huge traction engines towing their plough, and a caravan for the men to live in. Each traction engine had a winch with a long steel hawser, and the plough was a double six furrowed one. The engines were placed one each side the field, opposite each other. The cables from the winches were attached each end of the plough, then the plough was winched alternately from one side of the field to the other, the engines gradually moving forward.

The Botheridge family were all very talented engineers and traction engine drivers. They came from Norton, near Evesham, and settled in Campden. I can remember when I was quite a small boy, Chipperfield's came into the Square with their shows. They had a lovely big Showmen's Traction Engine; all polished brass on it. When it was time to move out, their engine broke down. Their own people tried, but couldn't get it going, so eventually they fetched old Charlie Botheridge, who was then well over eighty years old. They stood him on a box, and two men held him up whilst he worked. After about half an hour old Charlie says, "Right, you can get me down now, everything's alright." I don't know how much they gave him, but they were relieved, and thought the old man was marvellous.

After the war ended, farmers began to buy their own agricultural tractors, so the lovely steam ploughing outfits were gradually phased out, and unfortunately the same thing applies to the farm horses. Still, that's what we call progress.

Every Spring the great big shire stallions, and of course the "half legged" or lighter dray-type stallions, could be seen with their plaited manes and gay ribbons travelling from village to village. They really were a picture to look at, but now, alas, they were coming to an end.

These days we hold harvest festivals in most churches and chapels, but when I was a schoolboy, the schools, the choir, and clergy used to gather in a field up the Hoo every Rogation Sunday in May, and a service was held to bless the crops and pray there would be a good harvest. I think this custom came to an end when Canon Hitchcock retired [1934].

The Reverend Hitchcock must have been quite a wealthy man. He kept a gardener, whose wife was housekeeper, and there were also two servant girls. He used to travel around in a pony and trap, and I remember one time the Vicar and his wife were going down Aston Hill when, for some reason, the pony shied. The trap wheel went up onto the

24

high bank, and the trap turned over. Fortunately, neither the Vicar or his wife were hurt very badly.

Mrs. Hitchcock was one of the tallest ladies I have ever known, must have been well over six feet, and very thin. She always wore a very long, drab-looking dress, with an old grey cloak, and always seemed to be in a hurry: We always referred to her as "the Galloping Hairpin."

For one hour every week the Vicar came to school to teach us Religion. On one occasion I was reading a Buffalo Bill story, held under the desk. I must have got too enthralled with the story, he twigged what I was doing, and made me go out in front of the class and read a lesson out of the Bible to them.

About 1922 Canon Hitchcock had a new curate come, the Rev. W.A. Badger. Being a single man, he lodged with Mr. and Mrs. Walter Weale at Hulland House in Station Road. He soon became very popular, especially with the younger people. Realising there were no facilities in Campden to get youths off the streets, he formed a committee and persuaded Mr. Scudamore Griffiths to let them have a couple of rooms on the ground floor of Bedfont House. The public responded well by subscriptions and gifts of games, such as bagatelle, table tennis, darts, card tables and cards, etc. They formed a very good football team, of which my brother was captain and played centre forward.

Whenever Campden had a curate who became very popular they never seemed to stay long. Perhaps the Vicar got a little jealous: who knows? Anyway, the Rev. Badger had to move on, and the St. James Club gradually fell through. I think the Parish Council should have done something about it.

Between Jack Coldicott's Butcher Shop and Tom Hayden's Blacksmith Shop lived Miss Betty Hancock and her brother Steve. He, poor fellow, was - putting it mildly - very eccentric. They were both getting on in years, and she kept a small general stores. It was only through her efforts and generosity that we ever had a Christmas party. Each year in the Town Hall we had a real good tea, and as each child left they were given a penny and an orange. It must have been a sad loss to quite a few around the district when dear old Betty died. One in particular was old Sykes; there was always a cup of tea and something to eat when he called. Of course, all the older people knew Charlie Seitz ("Sykes") when he was a fine, clever young man, who took part in several amateur dramatic productions in Campden when he was with Doctor Morris.

Living at Tiltapin, or as some call it, Pike Cottage - that is the thatched house on the corner of Sheep Street and Catbrook - was

Wentworth Huyshe and his wife, who was the mother of those talented brothers, George, Will and Fred Hart. She also had two daughters and a son by Mr. Huyshe[*].

Mr. Huyshe had been a journalist all his life, one of the leading foreign correspondents in Fleet Street. He was also the gentleman who discovered the Izod family pedigree amongst the Harleian Manuscripts in the British Museum.

When I was about eleven years old, Mr. Huyshe wrote and produced a play called "The Brigands". It was the story of an attack on a British settlement by a horde of mounted dervishes. It took place in the Coneygree, and really was a magnificent spectacle. I have no idea of the number who took part, but I'm sure it must have been well over a hundred. I have always thought what a shame that it was never filmed. It was such a success that they had to give a repeat performance in Welcombe Park, Stratford-on-Avon. My father took part in it.

About this time Fred Merriman, a native of Broad Campden, retired after twenty-five years' service in the London Metropolitan Police. He bought a house in Kitchen Lane, Broad Campden. He had only been back a few days when crossing the road near Sheep Street he was knocked down by a bicycle. He was not hurt, but when he regained his feet he said, "Would you believe it, I've walked the streets of London for the past twenty-five years, and get knocked down by the first bloody swede-basher I see."

He had not been here long before he and some of the Hathaway family, with Fred Taylor, formed an orchestra. They called themselves "The Bijou Orchestra". For quite a number of years they were very popular at dances throughout the district. One evening each week they used to hold their band practice in the Infants School. It was quite usual to see a gathering of people outside on the pavement listening.

Campden always had a good brass band. For a good many years the conductor was Mr. Jimmy Pyment. He came to Campden with the Guild of Handicraft. During the summer months they were kept busy attending fêtes, clubs, etc., and if it was a nice evening, they would play

---

[*] *George and Will Hart came to Campden with the Guild of Handicraft, the one as a silversmith, the other as a wood carver, and both stayed after the Guild broke up to play a major role in Campden life. George's son Henry was also a silversmith, as is his son David who carries on the family business in the Silk Mill at the same benches as his father and grandfather did. George's other son, George junior, played Jethro Larkin in the Archers, the well-known BBC radio programme.*

for a couple of hours in the Square.

Occasionally they went to brass band contests in the Midland area. On one occasion they had been successful, and on the way home had called and celebrated at several pubs, arriving back at Campden very late at night. Before they got to Wolds End, they asked the driver to stop, saying they wanted to march down through Campden to let the people know they had won the contest. Then one or two said maybe it was a bit late, and the people may not like being awakened, so "Warrior" Smith said, "Well, in that case, we'll take our shoes off, and march down in our socks." Anyway, their "Victory" march was abandoned.

During the Great War Tom Hooke used to come to Campden and stay at the George and Dragon. About 1922 he married the landlord's daughter, Nell Smith. They bought the two houses where we lived, the cottage at the rear, and where Millett's bicycle shop was, the opposite side of the passage. They came to live in the house next door to us, and carried on with the bicycle business.

Mr. Hooke was quite badly crippled, both his legs and one of his arms being affected. He had been a comedian in London, and often appeared around here for charities. He formed "Tom Hooke's Jazz Band"; they were a scream, about eight of them in comic dresses, and all sorts of "instruments". For some years they were in great demand at fêtes, etc. I feel sure, if they could be seen now on television, they would be a hit.

One year there was a big sports meeting taking place in Pool Meadow; it included athletics, bicycle races, several horse races, and all the fun of the fair. To start the proceedings, Tom Hooke got a pal of his down from London to do a stunt: He was put in a trap in St. Catharine's Square, blindfolded with a black cloth - anyone was invited to inspect the blindfold - then he whipped the horse to a gallop, up the High Street, Church Street, down Calfs Lane to Town Mill, through the gate, across Cotterill's Orchard and into Pool Meadow. Obviously there was a trick in it, but the crowds who lined the streets were thrilled.

All the people who were present will never forget the finish of the principal horse race. Over the last quarter of a mile Scarrot's horse from Stow-on-the-Wold and Mr. Ambridge's horse from Milton-under-Wychwood were leading the others, locked neck and neck. Approaching the winning post Scarrot's jockey struck the other jockey several times across the face with the riding whip. Everyone could see it was quite deliberate. "Butcher" Jack Coldicott, who was on duty as a mounted steward, chased Scarrot's horse and jockey out of Pool Meadow, across Cotterill's Orchard, up through the Lygon Arms yard, into the High

27

Street, slashing the jockey several times across the back with his horsewhip. Of course from the crowd's point of view it was all very exciting.

When I was about twelve years old, and until I left school, every Saturday morning I went up the George and Dragon Yard to the house at the top in Back Ends, where there were two sisters lived. They were Sally and Ethel Hands, the middle-aged daughters of "Winket" Hands, who had farmed at Court Piece Farm. My job was to scrub the kitchen floor, then go part of the way down the Dragon Yard and scrub the wooden lavatory seat. That, I can assure you, was often a "lick and a promise". Their loo was quite a distance from the house - you had to walk down past four cottages to get there. The cottages were demolished in the 1930s.

Ethel Hands, the youngest sister, was very highly strung and eccentric, but Sally was a very kind and nice person. They had a good row once when I was there, and Ethel lost control of herself and started throwing the crockery about. I made a hasty withdrawal, and went to clean the loo seat. Not long afterwards, Ethel was put into a "home" near Gloucester. A couple of years later Sally married a Mr. Smedley who came to work at the chemist's shop. They left Campden and settled at Somerton in Somerset.

One of the highlights of the year was the annual meet of the North Cotswold Hounds at the Fish Inn every Boxing Day. The Master then was "Barney" Scot from Buckland Manor, a huntsman who was very popular with the gentry and the foot followers. People used to flock there from miles around. I should think Mr. Cottrel, the landlord, made enough money that day to keep him for months.

After the hounds had gone, there was rabbit coursing in the neighbouring field. Here you could back your dog against anyone who thought they had a faster one. This would go on for three or four hours, until eventually they ran out of rabbits. The rabbits had been ferreted out into purse nets previously. It was very cruel, really, and of course would not be tolerated these days.

I am sure the police turned a "blind eye" on drunks on these occasions, provided there was no violence. Of course there was the occasional argument which ended in blows, but that added to the crowd entertainment.

My father and other men have told me of the time a fight was arranged there between Uncle Bob and a man from Broadway named Joe Emms. It wasn't a hate fight, but just to prove who was best man -

there probably was betting on it. After a hard fight, which went on for quite a long time, Joe Emms admitted defeat. They shook hands whilst the crowd clapped and cheered them. Some time later, at Stow Fair, Uncle Bob challenged the Negro heavyweight in Jack Scarrott's Boxing Booth, and knocked him out; and at Stratford Mop later on in the year Uncle Bob wanted to take him on again, but they wouldn't accept the challenge. Jack Scarrott wasn't going to lose another five pounds.

Whenever any of us lads had a fight it was always a fair fight, and if there was a gang, the others would usually form a circle and watch, but they definitely would not interfere. But I'm afraid these days they have no sense of fairness, they will gang up on you, and if you go down, they very soon put the boot in.

I remember having a scrap with "Pecker" Howell outside the Armoury; we were both about twelve years old. We both had bloody noses, but in the end Pecker ran off home and left his cap on the ground.

There was one well-known bully named Geoff Harris. He was always known as "Goggles". He was about five or six years older than me, and for some reason which I can't remember he clouted me. So I got stuck into him, and was holding my own until he deliberately hit me in the pit of the stomach (a favourite trick of his). I had to gasp for breath, and was sick. He, in the meantime, ran away. When I told my brother, he said "Don't worry, I'll sort him out." The next day he caught Goggles visiting his girlfriend in Back Ends, and gave him a damn good hiding.

Looking back on my schooldays I often think how lucky I was to be able to get home for my mid-day meal. All the children from Broad Campden and the outlying farm cottages had to bring sandwiches, some of them like door-steps with a thin scraping of lard on. There was no such a thing as thermos flasks then, so if they wanted a drink, it meant a glass of water.

In the winter there was only one round coke stove to keep the school warm. No wonder some lads came to school wearing puttees, to keep their legs warm. Mother always made me wear a "gansey" in the cold weather; it was a navy blue pullover which buttoned up with four buttons up one shoulder. I hated the thing, because there were no pockets in it.

Down the Station Road at the Oddfellows' Ground were the school gardens. It was a half an acre divided into plots. They were allocated out, two boys to each plot. The other lad on my plot was Harry Bradley, who came from a very poor family who lived down Broad Entry, opposite the old convent. We used to march down there on Wednesday afternoons, providing, of course, if the weather was fine. All the seeds were provided, and you could take home what you grew. I let Harry Bradley have the produce off our plot; his mother was glad of it, and we were never short of vegetables at home.

All the tools were kept in a huge padlocked box, and I remember on one occasion when Boss Dewey went to unlock the box, some filthy devil had done "number two" right beside the padlock. Well, we had great difficulty trying to keep straight faces. Old Dewey could see that, and he flew into a violent temper, called us all "Campdenite Pigs", and said none of us would ever be any good except to follow the plough. He marched us straight back to school, and gave us a lesson on algebra; he knew we hated that.

On another occasion we were all sat under the wall of Griffiths's garden down Calfs Lane, drawing an old doorway leading into the rear of the Court House. Down the lane came Jack "Ripper" Keen from Broad Campden with a cider bottle in each pocket. It was obvious he was drunk. He stopped in front of Boss Dewey, stared down at him, and said, "You've got a f-----g good job, Boss." At that Boss Dewey started getting to his feet, and old Ripper ran down the bank with the Boss after him. We all shouted "Go on Jack", but Boss Dewey didn't pursue him very far.

I have never seen a man in such a temper. He seemed to be foaming at the mouth, and his moustache was quivering (this was always a bad sign). When he managed to get his voice back, he ordered us all back to school, and we had to stand with both arms in the air for twenty minutes.

I remember I hurt my heel once. I could not wear a shoe for a few days so had to go to school with a slipper on my right foot. During the eleven o'clock break one morning, we were at play in the playground when Mr. Dewey came walking up through towards the latrine. I went behind him pretending to kick him on the backside. I evidently overdid it, for my slipper fled off, missed the "old boy's" ear by a fraction, and finished up in the guttering. Of course he tumbled to what I had done, so that was another six on each hand. Another time I drew a rude picture of him and passed it across the gangway to Harry Pope. I never intended him to pass it back to me: as he was doing so, old Boss suddenly turned and saw him. When he saw the drawing with his name on it, the old moustache started quivering again, and out we had to go, another six on each hand.

There is no doubt about it, he enjoyed punishing you. I know I had my share, many times I have sat on my hands to cool them down and take the sting out of them. But I always thought he was a little scared of me during the last twelve months of my schooling; I was big and strong for my age, and he definitely eased up considerably on the caning. Times I have seen boys "pee" themselves when they have had to go out in front for punishment. On looking back, I have often thought what a gang of savages we would have been, if we would have had a weak teacher.

During the last fourteen months at school, I went down to Mr. Pyment's workshop every Thursday afternoon for carpentry classes. There were eight from our school, and eight from the Roman Catholic. Sometimes Mr. Pyment himself took the class, and sometimes Mr. Wall, who was cabinet maker at Pyments. We always preferred Mr. Pyment - Bill Wall was a grumpy old so-and-so, with no sense of humour at all. If he caught you having a bit of fun, he would slap you across the backside with a piece of wood. Anything we made, we could bring home. We still use the knife-box I made; that is over sixty years ago.

One afternoon I quietly tied a paper tail on George Scrimshaw's jacket, never realising Jimmy Pyment was aware of what I was doing. When I had completed the job, he said "Well done. You have had your fun, now we will have ours." So he tied it on me, and forbid me to take it off - a case of the biter getting bit.

There was a dear old lady named Miss Drury lived in the end Almshouse, near the steps. She belonged to a well-known Cotswold farming family, and must have been very well educated, and had travelled considerably. Occasionally, one or two of us would visit her when we came out of school and ask her to show us the wing of the flying fish. This she kept in a large family Bible, and no matter how often we went she was always pleased to show it to us, and give us something to eat - usually some rice pudding.

When my brother Bill left school in 1918 he went to work for Colonel Paley, who lived at Cotswold House. Dick Hughes, who then lived in Flag Close Cottage, was gardener there at the time, and one of his daughters, Alice, was one of the maid-servants there. Alice later married George Plested. Bill helped in the garden, looked after and milked the jersey cow, and when the son came with his polo ponies, Bill helped with those. His wage was eight shillings per week.

The last eighteen months of my school days were spent at the Blue School. The Education Authorities had decided for economic reasons to have one mixed school, rather than separate Boys and Girls. Our Boys

31

School was closed, and we joined the girls at the Blue School. Mrs. Dewey was retired, and Mr. Dewey carried on as headmaster. Another teacher was engaged; she was a Miss Smith, and I think she came from somewhere near Birmingham. She was quite young, somewhere around twenty, and very attractive. Of course, us older lads thought she was "smashing", but Boss Dewey made her life a bit of a misery, really. Several times we have seen her almost in tears, and on one occasion she ran out of the school, and came back with the Rev. Hitchcock. We were all sent out into the playground for about half an hour. On returning, things carried on as though nothing had happened, but Miss Smith only stayed for about another three months.

There is one thing I must say about Mr. Dewey: He was very patriotic. We always had morning prayer, which always included a prayer for the welfare of Great Britain. Empire Day, May 24th, our school and the Roman Catholic School met at the War Memorial for a service and the singing of Empire songs. And, hard man as he was, I have seen the tears come into his eyes on these occasions.

One Saturday me, Bert Wilkes, and Charlie James were looking at my rabbits (tame ones) when Tom Hooke opened his back door, and said, "Come here, I want you three." We thought he wanted some help, but to our amazement he said, "I want you to listen to this." He had got a crystal wireless. We had to get right close to it, but we could distinctly hear an orchestra playing. I can't remember now, but I think it was the Savoy Hotel Orchestra. Anyway, that was the very first time we ever heard a wireless transmission. Later, when valve sets were being produced, Bert Wilkes and myself took a weekly magazine between us. It was called the "Wireless World". In one edition there was an advert, whereby if you sent one shilling, they would send you the blueprint and the instructions on how to build your own set, which was called the "Easy Change Three", meaning it was a three valve set. We decided we would send for it and have a go at building a set each, using our attic to work in.

We couldn't afford to buy the components all at once, so when we could afford some, we would cycle into Evesham on a Saturday, where there was a wireless supply shop, and get them gradually. When it came to soldering some of the connections, we had to get Alec Walker to do that for us. He was the son of the late "Sloshy" Walker from Berrington Mill, but was now living with his mother next door to Jesse Taylor's Photographic Shop near the Lygon Arms. He was very clever and talented with anything to do with wireless or electrics. I can remember he built a very powerful wireless once, took it up to Dover's Hill to test

32

it, and you could hear it quite plainly down in Campden. I think one of the large radio companies gave him a job in their laboratories, and he left Campden.

After about two years we decided that because Mother was deaf, we needed a more powerful set, so we bought a new twin speaker SuperVox. It was a good set, and when Mother died, Bill took to it. The set I made I sold to Bill Whalley, who worked for Uncle Bob. I only charged him three pounds, but I never had the money.

During the summer and early autumn, for those who were willing, there were plenty of opportunities to put a nice bit of money by to help out during the winter. I know I have gone bean or pea picking after school many times. It was fourpence for beans, and ninepence for peas. That was for twenty-eight pound bags. If it was good picking, I used to always pick at least three bags of peas after school. Anyone who didn't mind climbing ladders could earn a "fortune", starting off with the cherries, peas and beans, plums, damsons and apples. Some women always used to earn enough to buy new boots and shoes for all the family, and then still have a bit put by for winter.

The majority of the labouring class wives were certainly tough and hard working. You could always see them coming home with their old perambulators and hand-carts piled up with wood which they had gathered in Weston Park, and the lads as soon as they were strong enough would carry home a "shoulder stick".

Most Saturdays in the winter I used to go down to the gas works with our truck and bring back a large sack filled with coke. It was a shilling per bag, so the larger your bag the better.

Towards the end of 1919 the County Council decided to build four pairs of semi-detached houses with an acre of land to each house for ex-servicemen; a very good scheme. The contract was won by a firm from Berkeley near Gloucester. When the work started, my brother Bill left Colonel Paley's and got a job as carpenter's mate. From eight shillings a week he was earning fourteen - quite a large increase. The scheme was a boon to the local tradesmen, because owing to the war work had become very slack.

About this time, Bill Cutts, who was a very clever mechanic and had come to Campden as chauffeur etc. at the Noel Arms, decided to start up on his own and build a garage in the yard at the rear of the Red Lion. The foreman in charge of the Aston Road project was a Mr. Bates, and he contracted with Mr. Cutts to build his garage, which was to be of wooden construction. When the timber arrived on the site Walter Weale,

Harry Bricknell, my brother and one or two more were sent down to the Red Lion yard to erect the garage. Soon after the work was completed, detectives arrived at the Aston Road, and took statements from those who had worked on Mr. Cutts' garage. The foreman, Mr. Bates, who had just got married, was arrested, summonsed, and sent to jail, I think it was for six months. Apparently, everything to do with the construction of the garage, including the timber, had been booked to the Aston Road contract. All the workmen had been quite innocent as to what had been going on, but what a shock it must have been for Mr. Bates' new bride.

At Christmas 1924 my school days came to an end. Wilfred "Nunc" Smith, Charles "Halfpenny" Benfield, and Wilfred "Guthrum" Plested left at the same time. My nickname was "Tiger". I never knew why. Up until he died in 1985 "Oily" Wilkes always called me "Tiger."

Mr. Dewey also retired the same day. He made a short speech, and I got the impression it was a very sad day for him, and to our amazement he said he wished every success to the four young men who were leaving with him; a change from calling us "Campden Pigs", and only fit to follow the plough. For his retirement, Mr. Dewey had a new stone-built house erected by Pyments in Station Road, opposite the gate leading into the Coneygree. He certainly chose a lovely site, with a view looking across to Broad Campden Hill. The house is named Holmcote.

He had two sons, George and Percy. I don't remember George; I think he died in his teens. Percy was rather disabled with a club foot. He was very clever, particularly in chemistry, but a bit of a "ne'er do well", a great disappointment to his parents. He was also a great "leg puller". I remember one time when Charlie Wakeman became landlord of the Noel Arms, Percy ("Putty") Dewey worked for him brewing the beer. At the time the stables were being converted into sleeping quarters. Well, Percy got an old white "pee pot", painted round it in old English lettering "TOPIS SINTO", buried it in the earth where the floors were being excavated, and arranged it for one of the workmen to "find" it and fetch Mr. Wakeman. He carefully cleaned the dirt away, was quite convinced the words were in Latin, and called for Putty Dewey to come and look at it. It was quite a while before Wakeman realised the true meaning of the words on it.

During my schooldays, two or three times every year there would be a barrel organ, or as we called them, a "hurdy gurdy", would come around, sometimes with a monkey sat on top. They liked to play outside pubs and hotels because they knew they would come out with money just to get them to move on.

The circus was always popular. Every year one and sometimes two would come into Badger's Field. Fossett's and 'Lord' John Sanger's were two of the names I can remember who visited Campden several times. They were always sure of a "full house".

When I was about six years old there was a man came round with a large brown bear. It had a collar and chain attached to a pole, around which it was supposed to dance. I think the man and the bear stayed the night in the stables at the Red Lion.

Up until the early nineteen twenties the old bathing lake* was open each summer. To get there you had to go through Miller Keen's at Westington Mill. Old Richard Keen the miller lived with his sister Bessie. She was an old character, like someone out of one of Dicken's books in her old Victorian clothes and bonnet. She had a very bad cast in one eye; we used to say she had one eye in the pot, and one up the chimney. The bathing lake was open from Easter until the end of September, and if anyone attempted to go that way when it wasn't open, old Bessie was very soon out and turned them back.

One of Father's best friends was Charlie King, who kept a butcher's shop at Little Coxwell, a village near Faringdon. He was also a horse dealer, and kept quite a large kennel of greyhounds. One day when he was visiting us just after I had left school, he said would I like to go back with him for a holiday. Mother and Dad said they could manage, so off I went, and stayed about ten days. I had a lovely time. He took me with him to markets, visiting farms, and a coursing meeting at Wantage.

He had got a litter of greyhound puppies about nine weeks old, and the morning he brought me back home, he said because the mother of the puppies was a bitch he had bought from us, he would give me one of them; or, if I preferred, a fawn greyhound named Air Spring who was about seven months old. I chose Air Spring because he had already had his inoculations for distemper, etc. A few weeks later Uncle Bob said a friend of his was interested in buying a greyhound, would I sell Air Spring. I said I would. When he brought his friend the following week-end, it was Hector Smith from Offenham. After the usual bantering about the price, I let him go for twenty pounds.

A few days later Uncle Bob came to see me, and said Mr. Smith had phoned him to say he was very worried as the dog was quite ill. I went straight away down to Offenham on my bicycle. When I arrived there

* *Built by the Guild of Handicraft, and opened in August 1903.*

35

Mr. Smith had gone to Evesham on business, so his wife said, "You had better come and see Air Spring". Well, no wonder he was ill, he was in a small wooden shed with a paraffin heater going, also wearing a rug. I immediately took the heater out, told her to leave the rug on until the next day, and then discard that. Everything eventually turned out very well, for when he was old enough he won several races at the Coventry Greyhound Racing Track. A couple of years later Hector Smith bought another young greyhound from Father, but unfortunately it jumped off the back of one of his lorries and broke its leg.

Every Saturday four or five of us, but occasionally just Bert Wilkes and myself, cycled to Evesham to go to the pictures. When we first started going it was to the old silent film picture house in Swan Lane. The seats right up in the front were fourpence, and if it wasn't a full house, we used to creep back into the better seats when the lights went out. It could get very noisy in there when the exciting scenes came on, especially if it was a Western. When the talkies came a new cinema was built in the High Street, called the Scala. The old Swan Lane one didn't survive very long then. The first talkie we saw was Janet Gaynor in "Sunny Side Up", and the following week, George Arliss in "Disraeli".

I shall never forget the journey home one Saturday night. There was myself, Bert Wilkes, Wilf Plested, and Bert Keyte. We called in Poole's Fish and Chip Shop at the bottom of Bengeworth near the Workman Bridge, and bought a bottle of lemonade and some chips, then decided we would get as far as Aston-Sub-Edge, sit on the memorial at the foot of the hill and eat our chips. When we had eaten them it was about ten minutes to midnight, so we said if we hurried up the hill we would be there in time to see the "White Lady" [a local ghost] cross the road at the top. Walking up the hill, we kept talking about the ghost, and wondering if we should see it. As we came around the bend in the road at the top there in the right hand side of the road was something white. In an instant, without any warning, Bert Keyte turned around, jumped on his bike, and went back down the hill. We all shouted, but to no avail. The "apparition" turned out to be some Council tar barrels stacked there, with the ends painted white so that they could be seen. Bert Keyte told us the following day that he came home via Weston-Sub-Edge, but we had our suspicions that he went to his auntie's in Aston-Sub-Edge.

It was about this time that my brother left home. A friend of ours, Harry Jeffries, had been farm bailiff for a Mr. Pavey at Hemel Hempstead in Hertfordshire. Harry was leaving to get married, and recommended Bill for the job, which meant living in the house with Mr.

36

and Mrs. Pavey and their little boy. Bill was quite happy there until Hemel Hempstead was being developed as a new town, and the Development Corporation commandeered the whole farm. Mr. Pavey bought another place near Newton Abbott in Devonshire, but Bill wouldn't go with them because he was courting. His young lady's father was part owner and manager of a brick and tile works nearby, and he found Bill a job there.

In the Spring of 1925 Mrs. Bruce's niece Winnie Sees came to visit her for a few days. She used to pop in to see my mother every day, because apparently she was nursemaid to me, and used to take me out in my pram when she was in her teens. Bert Wilkes was her cousin, and she invited Bert and me to go and spend a holiday at her home in Colindale. We decided we would save up our money for the next few months, and take up her offer. Neither myself or Bert ever smoked or went to pubs, so that helped considerably. At the end of September off we went for a week. We travelled up to Paddington by train where Alf Sees, Winnie's husband, met us and took us on the underground to Colindale.

The following morning (Sunday) he took us again by underground to Aldgate East Station, and then we walked to Middlesex Street, which of course is commonly called Petticoat Lane. You can imagine what an experience it was to us two country lads. Alf Sees, who was a true-bred Cockney, knew quite a few of the stallholders personally. It was only just under twenty minutes on the underground from Colindale to the West End.

We wanted to see as much of London as we could, so we went up to town every day. I shall never forget going to the Zoo. We thought it was wonderful, particularly the reptile house, where we were lucky enough to go in at feeding time to see the very large breeds like pythons and boa constrictors fed with live rabbits and rats. Madame Tussaud's was another place we went around. On the Saturday we decided to go to Stamford Bridge to see Chelsea Football Club play Blackburn Rovers. We went to a Lyons Corner House at mid-day and had some food. When we came out we were walking along the street when a bus pulled up in the traffic with a sign on the front saying 'Chelsea Football Ground'. We dashed into the road, got the bus - it was a double decker - and went up the stairs onto the top. After travelling along a couple of streets the conductor came up the steps. He was thunderstruck when he saw us. He said, "What the hell are you doing up here?" When we told him we were going to Stamford Bridge to see Chelsea play, he said "We have been there and are now going back to the depot." Anyway, he was

37

a decent sort. He put us off at a bus stop and told us the number of the bus to get on. We arrived at the ground in plenty of time and saw what we thought was a wonderful match, which Chelsea won by two goals to one. Included in the Chelsea team were Alex James and Hughie Gallacher, both famous internationals, and for Blackburn Rovers another international fullback, Big Jock Hutton. I have always been a Chelsea fan ever since.

When I left school I sold my two tame rabbits and used the cub* for a couple of ferrets. They are very strange little animals, but if handled enough they can become quite affectionate. If you have a gill (female) you must breed from her, or she won't live very long. When she gives birth her young are completely hidden away under the straw, or whatever it is you keep in the cub. If you attempt to look at them, she will kill and eat every one.

I worked hard helping my Dad on the land, milking two cows, feeding the pigs, and exercising greyhounds, but I was very happy. Money did not worry me. I knew Dad and Mother would have given me their last halfpenny if necessary. I was never short of pocket money, could always get a few rabbits and sell them.

Another source of income for me was mole-catching. Old Bill Buckland showed me the ins and outs of mole catching, and to dry the skins. Jack Harris and myself got half a dozen traps, and we did very well financially. There were plenty of moles about, and any of the farmers were only too pleased for you to go into their fields. If you could locate a main run, especially where it went down to a stream or pond, you could be almost sure of catching one every day. When you caught one, you skinned it and nailed the skin out onto a board to dry out. You put the nails through where the feet were, so as not to damage the skins. When we thought we had sufficient we sent them off to the Western Fur Trading Company at Somerton in Somersetshire. They graded the furs and sent the money back, which used to go from seven pence up to one shilling each fur, according to the grade.

Bill Buckland, who taught me how to catch moles, was a true-bred Romany who left his nomad existence when he married a local girl, Rose Benfield, sister to Ben, Tom, and Bill Benfield.

During the time when the early mornings were light, Jack Harris and

* "A rabbit or ferret cub was a home-made oblong box, with the front half or two-thirds covered with wire-netting, and made up with a wooden door. The real name is 'hutch', but 'cub' is the old local Cotswold name."

myself, about once or twice every week, would go down the fields as soon as it was light with Father's gun and get a few rabbits to sell at about one shilling each. We were very fortunate and never got caught, but had some narrow escapes. One morning we were creeping around the corner of a hedge and there, hardly ten yards in front of us, was Dudley Haydon with a cow having a calf. We quietly withdrew without him seeing us. Another morning Len Potter chased us when we were down the Mivies. He kept shouting "Stop"; what a hope he had.

Father was now gradually becoming crippled up with arthritis. On two occasions he'd been to some baths in Droitwich for treatment, but they did not seem to be very beneficial really.

The Council took over the land at the Oddfellows for building Council houses, so we lost that.

The whole country seemed to be heading for a slump. It was getting quite common to send produce to market, and finish up in debt after you had paid carriage and auctioneer's fees. We had over forty Worcester Permain apple trees in the Big Ground. They were loaded with lovely apples, but they just would not pay for picking, and you could not store them, of course, because they are not a keeping apple. It was nearly as bad with the plums; we had quite a lot of Tsars and Monarchs. Uncle Bob did manage to get rid of those for us, but the profit was very small.

Ernest Woolliams, Dad's friend, had now taken Holt Farm on Northwick Hill, and he offered a good price for the two cows, so Dad let them go. He also took the cooling machine at the same time.

One evening, "Bummer" Haines, the local plumber, who was an old school pal of Father's, was paying us a visit when he turned to me and said, "I could do with a good strong lad like you for two or three months." Apparently, he had got the contract to put in a central heating and complete new sewage and draining scheme at Burnt Norton House for the Earl of Harrowby. Well, the outcome was, with Dad and Mother's permission, I took the job on at the rate of eight pence an hour. I started the following Monday with seven or eight others. Fred Bennett the plumber was in charge of the job.

The following morning Sam Byrd came to work with us. About ten o'clock old "Bummer" came on his motorcycle and sidecar; on seeing Sam, he shouted out "Oh, oh, we've got a 'bird' with us this morning." Sam shouts back, "Yes, and he is going to bloody well fly, if you don't give him another halfpenny an hour." They were a good gang of men to work with, and I enjoyed every minute of it.

Mr. Haines had a son named Harold, who was about six years older than me. He was a very clever fellow, but a little eccentric. He had been expelled from the Grammar School for sending an anonymous letter to the headmaster, Matthew Cox, threatening to blow the school up. Somehow, they recognised the writing and traced it to him.

About this time there was a lady named Mrs. Barrow who had bought Woolstaplers Hall. She brought her chauffeur with her. He was a tall, handsome-looking man named Charles Way. He lived in one of the cottages at the rear of the George and Dragon, by himself. He had a car of his own, an old Model T Ford, which he let out to anyone, provided they could produce a driving licence. Myself, Bert Wilkes and Bert Keyte decided we would like to learn to drive, so we each sent to Gloucester for a driving licence - cost five shillings, and no question of any sort of test then. Reg Howell, who was a couple of years older than we were, worked for Tom Hopkins the butcher at the time, and drove the van delivering the meat. We had a word with Reg and he agreed, if we hired the car on a Sunday, he would teach us to drive it. We did this for two Sundays. When we returned the car the second Sunday I straightaway booked it for the following Sunday, and drove Mum and Dad up to Hemel Hempstead for the day to see Bill. The weather was lovely, except for the wind: I can see Mum and Dad now with their scarfs tied round their heads to keep their hats on.

I'm sure that old Model T was a remarkable car. We gave it some rough usage, but it never once let us down. When you started you cranked it up on battery, and as soon as the engine was running you had to run round and switch it over to ignition. The accelerator was a lever on the steering wheel. There was a handbrake which operated on the back wheels, but the footbrake was connected to the transmission.

As far as anyone in Campden knew, Way was a single man, very "friendly" with a girl from Aston-Sub-Edge. But something happened, we never knew what, but he just left the district without any warning, and Joe Hedges - a Campden fellow - was Mrs. Barrows' chauffeur. Some years later, in November 1937, there was a report in the "News of the World" that Charles Sidney Way had shot himself at Clacton-on-Sea. There were three women at his funeral: his real wife, who he had deserted; his mistress, who had two children by him; and his sister. It was the first time they had ever met each other, and according to the newspaper, they each said how much they loved him, and each paid a third of the cost towards the funeral.

Any spare time I had was spent with Dad's greyhounds, and I well remember one summer's evening in the company of Jack Harris. We set off with four greyhounds up Dyers Lane and Long Hill, out on the London Road by the Pillars, along the main road to the Cross Hands, and down to Westington. When we had just passed the rubbish tip at Horseman's Corner we heard the most unusual chattering noise coming from Sam Gladwin's field. When we looked over the wall we could hardly believe our eyes - there was an "army" of rats, travelling up the field towards the rubbish tip. Jack and myself estimated that they covered an area quite twenty yards across by seven or eight yards deep. I would definitely think there must have been more than a thousand.

A few years later Alec Cooper had a frightening experience. Alec lived up the Aston Road, and though he wasn't a drinking man, he went to the Red Lion every evening for the company. When returning home one night on his bicycle he heard this chattering noise, and then saw this "colony" of rats coming towards him, taking up the whole of the road. He said he sat perfectly still on his bicycle, with one foot on the verge, whilst they scampered by. For a second or two he was completely surrounded. He said it was the most frightening experience he ever had in his life.

After I finished working for Bummer Haines, "Butcher" Jack Coldicott saw me and said he could do with a couple of strong lads for a few weeks, so me and Jack Harris went. Our first job was hoeing and cutting out sugar beet in Broadpath. One day, when it rained, he sent us over to clean out some calf pens at Broad Campden. There were three of us - myself, Jack Harris and Dick "Balsam" James. Where we were working was quite close to Hollybush, where old Geoffrey Smith was living after retiring from Attlepin Farm. During the morning Mr. Smith came across to us and said him and his wife were going out for the remainder of the day, but if we would like a drink of cider with our lunch, we could go and get some ourselves as there was a barrel in his shed at the rear of the house.

Jack Harris and myself, who were both teetotallers, didn't bother, but Dick, who liked his drink, went across when he knocked off at lunch time, and came back in quite a merry mood. About four o'clock off he went again, and this time when he came back he was staggering. I told him he had taken advantage of Mr. Smith's kindness, and ought to be ashamed of himself. He then turned quite nasty, swearing at me and threatening me with a pitchfork. I didn't like hitting him, because he was drunk, but he gave me no alternative. I knocked him down and took the fork off him. I didn't fancy it being stuck in my tummy.

Just before we finished for the day poor old Geoffrey Smith came over, white with temper - Dick had left the tap on the barrel turned on, and the floor of the shed was covered with cider. When Dick reported for work the following morning, Butcher Jack was waiting for him, and turned him off the farm.

I had quite a frightening experience one day. Butcher Jack bought a big cart horse from Bert Spencer, a farmer and horse dealer who lived at Draycott. He sent me with a wagon up to Horace Badger's farm at Lapstone to fetch a load of straw. Everything went well until I got to Conduit Hill. I stopped at the top and put the slide on one of the rear wheels, and started down the hill. I realised we were gradually increasing speed, and by the time I got to the bottom, me and the horse were running nearly as fast as I could go. Thank heaven the horse kept his feet; - if he had stumbled and fell, I dread to think what would have happened. The horse turned out to be what is known as a "rig". They can pull, alright, but due to a back weakness they cannot hold anything back. A few weeks later the horse was sold at Stow Fair.

I stayed on working on the farm until the harvest was gathered in and really enjoyed it, but of course the wages were only thirty shillings a week, and tenpence stopped out of that for insurance.

There is such a lot of talk and articles written these days about the bad old days. Well, I'm afraid I differ. To me, the world - or should I say, my world - the world I was brought up in, was a much more contented and peaceful place. I know there was some poverty, some of it due to the drinking habits of both the fathers and mothers. But there - the very same thing applies now-a-days; more so, in fact, because drugs have become a far larger problem than alcohol. What worries me these days is the attitude of Councils and so-called intellectuals in their belief that it is wrong to have discipline in schools; and also the number of left-wing teachers, who by devious means teach their political dogmas to the children.

Practically everybody years ago were very patriotic, but there are far too many these days whose only thought about their country is how much they can get out of it financially.

Although there was no such thing as a Health Service, the Benefit Societies were a boon to everyone. Nearly every public house had a Sick and Dividend Club, where you paid a sum each week, and then at Christmas you drew your money out, plus extra money made out of raffles, etc. If you had the bad luck to be ill during the year you had ten shillings sick pay for six weeks. After six weeks, it was cut down to five shillings.

These pub clubs were very helpful, but I don't think compared favourably with either the Stroud Mutual Benefit Society or the Cirencester Conservative Benefit Society. Both of these were very popular in Campden. Bummer Haines was secretary for the "Ciren", and Dickie Dunn, who was married to Bummer's sister, was secretary to the Stroud.

Although the "Ciren" had the word "Conservative" in its title, it was absolutely non-political.

I think they both had exactly the same rules. You paid in once a month, and any one person could hold up to ten shares. If you were sick you were paid ten shillings a week for each share, and any doctor's fees were also paid. If it was necessary they would pay the fee for a second opinion, or in some cases send you away for treatment, like the Stroud did for Father when they sent him to the brine bath at Droitwich. Your money, of course, accumulated over the years with the interest, but at the age of sixty-five you automatically ceased to be a member; but had a nice sum of money to come for your retirement.

I shall never forget one Saturday I cycled with Bert Wilkes to Evesham and went to the cinema. When we came out to go to Poole's Fish and Chip Shop, we picked up a couple of girls we had known before. This made us very late to start our journey home. It was a very dark night, and the oil lamps on our bicycles were not much of a help. We were coming down Horsebridge Hill without putting our brakes on when without any warning my front wheel hit something and over the top I went, onto my head. Bert said I was completely knocked out. He dragged me on to the footpath, and a vehicle appeared, coming down the hill. He stood in the road and stopped it. What a stroke of luck - it was Harry Blake, driving Jack Horne's van from Campden. We were nearly back at Campden before I came to. When I got up the following morning I had a lump on my forehead like a purple duck egg, and it hurt to turn my head around for several days. I reckon my skull must be as thick as old Slap Blakeman's.

About 1927 the old Campden Council decided that the brook badly needed cleaning out. There were no mechanical excavators, etc., then; it was a case of shovels and manpower. It was a case of temporarily employing extra labour, so me and Jack Harris decided to start. Beside us two there were George "Bungy" Dyde, "Slippy" Stanbrook, Billy Cherry, and Harry Griffin the roadman, who was in charge.

We started at the bottom of Pool Meadow near Berrington Mill. Fortunately, the weather was fine and warm right throughout. Really, we quite enjoyed it. Myself, Jack Harris and Bungy Dyde were much younger than the others, and we used to play them up a bit. Where the bed of the brook was soft, we would get in front, dig a hole quickly, then make the water very muddy so that they could not see the hole. Then in they would go, with the water filling their wellies. Poor little Billy Cherry and Slippy Stanbrook, who had very bad eyesight, took it all in good part, but old Harry Griffin used to get a bit nasty sometimes.

It was not long after this job had finished that I remember Bungy Dyde, who was a very heavy cider drinker, was summoned for assaulting Ted Pieters outside the Volunteer. Ted Pieters was a Belgian who had married "Smocky" Lee's daughter, Daisy. He was a very inoffensive man, and worked as a painter for Tom Parsons at Weighbridge House.

About this time there was a gang of teenagers who were always in trouble with the police. They were a couple of years older than me. They used to go to the pubs quite a bit, and then make themselves a nuisance at dances, etc. There was about five of them, and Charlie Nicholls seemed to be the ringleader. One Saturday night at a dance, Oily Wilkes, one of the gang, kept bumping into me quite deliberately, so I told him to lay off. He said, "Come outside, and I'll show you who is gaffer." Anyway, down we went into the Square, and all his cronies formed a circle round us. There were only two hits - I hit Oily, and he hit the ground. The next morning I was walking back from the lavatories and met poor old Oily going down; he had a lovely black eye. I couldn't help feeling sorry for him.

Not long after that it was my turn to have a black eye. There was a fête and sports to be held at the opening ceremony of the new Recreation Ground [1928]. Uncle Bob, who was on the Committee, was in charge of a stall. My brother was home for a couple of days, and that morning we had been sparring with the boxing gloves on, where we kept the greyhounds near Westington Mill. I hit Bill a bit harder than I should have done on the nose; he got into a temper, and for a time we really had a go. When we arrived back up home, there was a message from Auntie Lil saying Uncle Bob had been taken ill, would I run the stall in his place. Well, of course I couldn't refuse, but by the time the fête was due to be opened my eye had turned a lovely purple colour. Of course, Bill was laughing his head off.

When I was about sixteen, I went with Mr. Jeffries, who was breeder of greyhounds from Bledington, to take a greyhound he had sold to a gentleman at Bletchley, Buckinghamshire. After delivering the greyhound, Mr. Jeffries called in to visit Mr. T. G. Curtis, a very well known greyhound and polo pony breeder at Borough Farm, Newton Longville, Bletchley. Whilst showing us round his kennels, he had two little eight week old bitch puppies sired by his famous stud greyhound, Newville Captain, a winner of the Barbican Cup at Altcar. The man who bred them had brought them the day before, told Mr. Curtis he really couldn't afford the ten guineas stud fee, would he accept the two puppies instead. Mr. Curtis said he really hadn't kennel room for them, and would have to sell them. I asked him how much he would sell them to me for. He said, seeing that I was with Mr. Jeffries, who was a great friend of his, he would let them go for five pounds each. I told him I would have to consult with Father, so he said if he didn't hear anything for three days, he would have to advertise them. When I went home the following day and showed Father their pedigree, which Mr. Curtis had kindly written down, he sent a wire straight off and accepted the offer. Two days later a letter came from Mr. Curtis saying he was sending them in a special container by train. They arrived by passenger train at Campden Station, and had only been in the container just over an hour.

They turned out to be the fastest two greyhounds we ever had. They were registered in the Stud Book as "Campden Lady" and "Campden Lass". Campden Lady was just a shade the faster of the two, and the only time she was ever beaten was when she injured her shoulder at Dumbleton.

The first time they ran was at a meeting of the Lower Swell Coursing Club. I well remember that, for I walked to Fox Farm at Condicote with them, they both won their stakes, and thankfully I did not have to walk back: I rode back with Father in Tom Baldwyn's pick up. Mr. Baldwyn, who was farming at Hidcote, was Father's cousin.

After winning at Lower Swell, we took them to the Aylesbury Club's meeting at Kirtlington, where Campden Lady won the Kirtlington Park Stakes, beating in the final Mr. T.G. Curtis's Newville Collegian, which he thought was his best greyhound at that time. I remember he said to Father would he consider selling her, but knowing my Dad, I knew he wouldn't part with her at any price.

The next time that we took them to the Aylesbury Club's meeting, which was held at Cheddington Hill on the Mentmore Estate, Campden Lass was beaten in the semi-final and Campden Lady again was unbeaten. At the next meeting of the Lower Swell Private Club we ran Campden Lady, but she ran in the name of "Magic" and won the main event and a silver cup. Because it was a private club it was not necessary to enter her under her registered name, so to fox the bookmaker we entered her under the name of "Magic".

45

"Dad with greyhounds in the Leasows. 1928."

·GREYHOUND STUD BOOK·
CERTIFICATE OF TRANSFER

The following *five* Greyhounds, the property of *Mrs J R Coldicott*
The Squere   Campden   Glos
have been Registered in the Stud Book this *twenty fifth* day of *Sept* 192*9*

VOL. XLIX.
H. A. GROOM, 11, Haymarket, London, S.W. 1
No. of Certificate A 844
Keeper of Greyhound Stud Book by Authority of the National Coursing Club

No.	Name of Greyhound	Colour	Sex	Sire	Volume	Dam	Volume	When pupped
	Beaded Lass	w bk	b	Beaded Dan	(42)	Campden Lass	(45)	June 1928
	„ Ellen	bd	b	Do.		Do.		Do.
	„ Flirt	bk	b	Do.		Do.		Do.
	Campden Lass	w bk	b	Nevrville Captain	(39)	Leighton Flirt	(40)	Mar 1926
	„ Lady	bk	b	Do.		Do.		Do.
				Transferred to F Haines & renamed Black Beaded Flirt 28/3/30				

You are requested to satisfy yourself that the above entries are correctly made, and if any
alteration is required, to return this Certificate with instructions at once.

Registration Fee 2/- ____ received

46

We didn't run Campden Lass at this meeting because Father decided to breed from her. At Lower Breeding, near Horsham in Sussex, Sir Woodman Burbridge, who was the then owner of Harrod's Stores in London, had his kennels. There he had a stud dog named Beaded Dan, so Father wrote and booked a nomination for Campden Lass. When she was in season, a friend of Father's, Mr. Drinkwater from Kingham, took me, with her, in his car. Everything went well. It was really quite an experience. The kennel manager asked all sorts of questions about the bitch, and because she was a virgin bitch he smeared his finger with vaseline and "probed" her first before he led the dog out.

Another experience I shall never forget was when she whelped. It was about eleven o'clock at night, and I sat in the kennel with her talking to her. She had two dogs and three bitches. As each puppy arrived they seemed to be encased in a skin. This she gently nipped with her teeth, pulled off, and ate it, and it was marvellous to see her push them with her nose towards her breasts.

About this time there was a firm from Liverpool called British Insulated Cables came to Campden to put the electric main cables through the streets. The local councils had insisted (quite rightly) that there should be no overhead cables anywhere in a built up area* .

They erected an office and store-shed opposite Sheep Street. I went there and saw the foreman, a little man in a bowler hat. He said I could start work the following morning. There must have been at least a dozen men there the next morning. I was definitely the youngest, but I was very strong then, and knew I would cope alright. The foreman and his son marked the line of the trench, and then each man had his section, which was three lengths of a pick-axe handle. It was hard work. The old foreman was walking up and down the whole time. The pay was one shilling an hour, which was two pence halfpenny an hour more than the local rate.

The second morning when I was going to work, old Ted Ladbrook the

* *Since appearing in Christopher Whitfield's "History of Chipping Campden", published in 1958 (see page 252), it has often been said that the electric and telephone cables were run into Campden underground because of the unheralded efforts of F.L. Griggs, the internationally known artist and benefactor of Campden. Local newspaper coverage of the time makes it clear, however, that Mr. Coldicott is correct, and that it was members of the parish council who took the initiative in a successful campaign to have the cables run underground. Contemporary press reports suggest that the Post Office may never actually have had any intention of bringing overhead telephone lines into Campden anyway.*

47

butcher was stood outside his shop; he said, "Well, Master Coldicott, how are you getting on?" So I showed him my hands, which were sore and blistered. He said, "Hang on a minute, I'll put something on them." He came back with a jar of ointment of his own making. He rubbed plenty on my hands and told me to see him again the following morning, which I did. What ever the concoction was, it was marvellous. He also told me I was gripping the pick-axe handle too hard. After a couple of days I had no further trouble.

On the Friday we had to queue in a row at the office for our pay. As you got to the lid-hole you gave your name, and they handed you your packet. There was a notice saying you must check if it was correct straightaway, and when I checked mine I had a pound too much, so I joined on the end. When I got to the lid-hole, I gave my name and said I had a pound too much. He said, "Well, then, you're bloody lucky, buzz off, do you want to get somebody in trouble." I very soon disappeared.

After the underground contract was completed, a new foreman was sent to erect the overhead cables from Campden to Moreton-in-Marsh. He was quite a young man, named Bob Smith. He didn't want any older men in his gang, as it entailed a lot of walking, digging out the holes for the poles which were to carry the cables. When the poles were erected as far as Moreton, the Electricity Board's linesmen came to put up the power cables, so I carried on with them as a linesman's mate. I could have carried on beyond Moreton; they wanted me to, but it was too much travelling.

Not long after, I met Bob Smith again. He had just married Gracia Jeffries from Bledington. She was a friend of mine, who I had flirted around with on and off - she was the daughter of the Mr. Jeffries who I was with when he took me to Mr. Curtis's at Newton Longville. Anyway, Bob wanted me to go with him to south Wales, where he was going in charge of a large contract, but with Father unable to work then I couldn't have left home.

Whilst working on the powerline between Campden and Moreton I got quite friendly with Jack Wheatcroft from Draycott, no relation to the Ebrington Wheatcrofts. At that time I had a couple of good ferrets: A black and white gill (black and white ones were known as "fitchers"; she was the best ferret I ever had, I could carry her inside my shirt and she would lie there and never move); the other was a dog ferret, which I used as a "liner". After you put your first ferret in, and for some reason or other nothing happened, you then used your liner. He wore a very small collar with a long line attached. Every yard on the line was a knot, so that you knew how far in it went, and if it came to a case where you had to dig out, you could follow the line. Anyway, what I was going to say was, I was fool enough to lend my ferrets one weekend to Jack Wheatcroft, and he lost my little fitcher. I was upset - I knew I should never have another as good as she was. I went over to Draycott and made him show me where he had lost her. He had put her into a large warren under a large elm tree. I'm afraid I told him what a b----y fool he was to put a single ferret in such a place, and that he was very lucky he had not lost them both. (End of friendship).

I remember one year, I think it was 1927, a film company arrived in Campden to make some scenes for a film called "The King's Highway". It caused great excitement; everyone who was not working turned out to watch. I remember the part of the Highwayman was played by a famous actor named Matheson Lang, but I'm afraid I have forgotten the name of the leading lady. The "Highwayman" came dashing down the passage at the Baptist Chapel, with the Bow Street Runners in hot pursuit, and I also remember the heroine coming along the High Street in an old stage coach.

There was a terrible tragedy in May 1929. Dick Green, who was a plasterer working for Espley's at Evesham, lived with his wife and little boy Tommy in one of the council houses in Aston Road. Tommy, who was eight years old, and Roland Dyer, his little playmate, went bird-nesting in the fields the opposite side the road. Tommy climbed a tree overhanging a small pond, and fell out of the tree into the pond. Poor little Roland Dyer raised the alarm, but when help arrived little Tommy was beyond help. He was such a lovely looking and popular little boy, their only child. A terrible tragedy.

At this time my father, who hadn't been able to work for some time, had to take to his bed. After a few days his breathing was gradually getting difficult, and Doctor Davis decided he had pneumonia. As well as giving him the doctor's medicine, Mother was keeping him supplied with hot water bottles. His sister, Mrs. Hiatt from Quinton House, brought him a large jar of calves foot jelly, and his other sister, Mrs. George Haines, brought a bottle of brandy and fruit.

On the Saturday of Scuttlebrook Wake, after tea, I went and sat on the bed talking to Dad, and he seemed very much better and his voice was stronger. He said to me, "You go up to the Wake and enjoy yourself. I am much better, and will be alright." So later on I did go up, and told Mother I would not stay out late. I hadn't been up there hardly an hour when Charlie Ladbrook tapped me on the shoulder and said, "You're wanted down home immediately." I knew straight away what had happened. I ran all the way home, and there was Mother, Mrs. Tom

Hooke, and Mrs. Bruce crying their eyes out. I ran upstairs and put my ear on Father's chest. I just could not believe it.

At that time Father's greyhounds - I think there was eleven then - were in some kennels in the field next to Westington Mill. When I went down to feed them the morning after Father died the people in Deben Cottages and other houses nearby asked me what was the matter with the greyhounds, as just after ten o'clock the night before they had howled and made such a terrible noise for about a quarter of an hour. When I told them that Father had died at that same time they were astounded. I have always been convinced that they knew of his death. It was a great blow to me. He thought the world of me, and I loved him dearly.

The widow's pension in those days was only ten shillings a week, so I realised I should have to get a regular job, and that meant getting rid of the greyhounds. I sold one of Campden Lass's saplings to Hector Smith, and one to Mr. Haines from Wick near Pershore. I gave Campden Lady to Father's friend, Mr. Charlie King, the butcher at Little Coxwell; I knew Dad would never have sold her under any circumstances, and she would have a good home with Mr. King. He said he would breed from her, and if at any time I should want another I could have the pick of his kennel. All the others I entered for a sale of greyhounds at Aldridge's Repository, in London. At that time Jack Horne had got quite a large van, so I hired Jack and his van and took them to the sale at Upper St. Martin's Lane, London. It was heartbreaking to let them go, but I'm afraid I had no option.

Old Bert James, who lived in one of the cottages in Lane's Yard at the rear of our house, had worked as scaffolder for Pyments from the very start, when Jimmy Pyment opened the business. After we buried Father, Mr. James told me that although the building trade was rather quiet at the moment, he would see if, with his recommendation, Pyments would set me on. A few days later he arranged for me to go to Pyments' office for an interview. They questioned me as to what work I had done previously, and what rate of pay did I have on my last job. When I said one shilling per hour, Mr. Harold, the eldest of the two brothers, said "You can start with us, but we can only pay you nine pence halfpenny per hour," which was the normal rate at the time for builders' labourers.

I started work for them the following Monday morning at 7 o'clock, at Mr. Arthur Watkinson's, Maidenwell, Broad Campden. The contract was to excavate for, and build, a private swimming pool. All the excavation had to be done by pick, shovel, and wheelbarrow. We were quite a large gang: I can remember there was Jackie Webb, Frank

Bennett, "Fag" Turner, Jim James, Ernest Hedges, Bill White, Charlie Pitcher, and myself. We were the labourers. George Plested and Jack Pitcher were the two tradesmen, that is, masons or bricklayers. On looking back, I am the only one still alive.

Mr. Arthur Watkinson was quite a rich man, a practicing Roman Catholic. He was unmarried, but for some years Mrs. Arthur Bunting lived with him as housekeeper. Arthur Bunting was a half brother to Harold and Arthur Pyment, and worked with William (Bill) Wall in the cabinet makers' workshop. "Bunt" was a hell of a nice man, always jolly, just the opposite to Bill Wall, who was very dour, and had no sense of humour. Bunt was a good Bandsman, and played in Campden Town Band under his step-father Jimmy Pyment for many years.

I always thought Watkinson was a "spineless" and eccentric type of man. At Maidenwell there were quite a number of damson trees, and every year, with the help of his gardener Jim Ashwin, he would make a considerable amount of damson wine, and nothing delighted him more than to get people "tipsy", particularly the Town Band. He would invite them over on a week-end and keep their glasses well filled, knowing that several of them who were drinkers would end up making fools of themselves.

After the swimming pool at Maidenwell was completed, the job I went on was at Campden Parish Church. The pinnacles and battlements on top of the tower needed some repair work. Old Bert James the scaffolder, with me, Frank Bennett, and Ernest Hedges to help him, were sent to erect the scaffolding ready for the masons to do their work. There was no modern scaffolding then. All we had were poles, ropes and pudlocks. Pyments had sent away for a special extra-long strong rope for the job, because everything had to be pulled up from the outside on a pulley. Although Mr. James was then well over sixty, he stood out over the side of the tower on a single nine-inches-wide plank, fixing the wire rope to the over-hanging pole to which the pulley wheel was to be hung. To secure the wire rope he had to use both hands, so could not hold on to anything to keep his balance. He was a very remarkable man.

I was never scared of heights, and I think Mr. James realised this because he always asked for me when there was any scaffolding to be done.

Before I go further, I think I ought to explain what "pudlucks" were: They were 5 feet long lengths of timber, about 5 inches by 4 inches, usually made of ash, and they were used as bearings to support

51

the planks on a scaffold.

It was about this time, I can't remember the date, there was a disastrous farm fire at Will Haines's, Westington. Apparently, it was the worst in the Campden Parish since my grandfather Robert Coldicott's fire, also at Westington, in 1874. At both these fires there was an acute shortage of water, and in both cases again cider was used, but to no avail. Three barns were badly damaged, and the estimated value was around £2,000.

Where the brook (now "river" Cam) passes under the road between the railway and the Paxford turn, the culvert was considered by the County Council to be unsafe, so Pyments were given the contract to put in a new culvert. This meant doing half the road at a time, and for a few nights it meant having a night watchman on duty, Mr. Pyment left it to us workmen to make out our own rota; none of the older men seemed very happy about doing the Saturday night, so I said I would do that one. There was a small hut and a brazier with some coke and coal. We had an old iron kettle there, so I took some milk, sugar, tea and sandwiches. Just before midnight a girl from Charingworth named Cadell came on a bicycle. She had been to a dance at the Town Hall in Campden. Anyway, I made her a cup of tea and shared my sandwiches with her. We sat talking for half the night, so the night didn't seem so long after all.

Not long after this I was sent, with a tradesman named George Eden from Blockley, to carry out various repairs to the buildings at Snake Bank on the Campden House Estate. They are farm buildings with the wood either side of them, and there were quite a few pheasants about at that time. The keeper, a man named Mr. Oakey, lived in Tilborough Cottage. I thought, "Somehow, I've got to have some of those pheasants whilst we are here", so one afternoon I filled a sack bag with chaff, etc., which I swept up off the floor of the farm buildings. The next morning I dismantled my gun, put it in a bag, and took it with me; but instead of going through Campden Wood, I went on up Dyers Lane, and along by Weston Park, and down the field to the buildings. Then I took the bag of chaff about twenty or thirty yards into the woods and emptied it into a heap. George Eden said, "You idiot, you will never get away with it." It wasn't too long before there were six or seven pheasants pecking away. It was just a nice range for the pellets from the cartridges to spread and also not damage them too much; I never liked anything shot about too hard. Anyway, I'd bagged two and another badly hit trying to struggle away; I was over the fence in a flash, grabbed the three, and back to the buildings. The dutch barn was full of straw boltings (they didn't have bales then). We had got a good ladder there for roof repairs, so I quickly

Taken when I was 14 years old. 1927.

Top left: "My Grandmother, wife of Charles Izod. She was Elizabeth Carter from Childswickham."

Top right: "Grandfather Charles Izod. A dairy farmer, his dairy was in the High Street, where the Bantam Tea Rooms are. He delivered milk around Campden."

Left: "My Mother."

Top left: "Grandmother Juliana Baldwyn."

Top right: "Grandfather Robert Coldicott. Born 1834 at Bretforton. Married Juliana Baldwyn at Ashton-under-Hill in 1858. Farmed at Hinton-on-the-Green. Moved to Westington Home Farm in 1868. They had four sons and four daughters."

Right: "Father with large hat [centre]. Tom Haines right. Canada 1903."

Jim "Teapot" Wilson

Charlie Sykes (Seitz)

put it up against the straw, put the gun and the birds on top of the straw, and pulled the ladder down. I knew if I had hidden them near the ground the gamekeeper's dogs would smell them out. Sure enough, it wasn't long before old Oakey appeared. He said, "Did you chaps hear a shot?" We said, "Yes, we thought it was you." I'm sure he was very suspicious, because he wandered around with his spaniel for quite a while. I was very fortunate, because later-on our lorry came to bring us some materials, so I told Bert Andrews, the driver, I would give him a drink if he would drop the gun and birds in to our house, which he did. I wanted George Eden to have one of the birds, but no way, he wouldn't. When we were cycling home through Campden Wood old Oakey was walking along; if I had had a bag he would soon have wanted to know what was in it: All's well that ends well. A few months after, George Eden emigrated to Australia.

The head of the police now was Superintendent Bert Bunker. He and Bill, his brother, and two sisters were old friends of my mother's. When they were young their father, Sgt. Bunker, lived at the police station, and so naturally they were all playmates. Now I was nineteen and big and strong and Bert Bunker tried hard to get me to join the police. He said, "Don't bother about the County Police. I'll tutor you for a while, and I'm positive you can get into the Birmingham City Police." Mother, quite naturally, was very upset at the thought of me leaving home, and I personally couldn't bear the thought of town life, so I turned it down. Was I right or not, I often wonder?

Charingworth Chase came up for sale, and it was bought by a very wealthy American lady who was residing there. Her name was Mrs. Pearce. She bought Charingworth Chase for her eldest son Jimmy Pearce, who had just married the former wife of Lord Inverclyde, from whom she was divorced. Her maiden name was Miss Olive Sainsbury, a member of the large grocery empire. Pyments were engaged to put up several loose boxes for the hunters, as well as carrying out alterations to the house.

They had a complete new central heating system installed. The contract for this was given to a firm from London; they sent down two plumbers, and I was loaned to them to knock holes through walls, make good again after the pipes were put through, or anything else that needed doing. I wasn't really happy working with them: You can have your Cockneys, give me a good old countryman any time. In the dining room and lounge there was a silver box of cigarettes kept on a table; these two plumbers never smoked so much in their lives, I'll bet. I heard the butler say one day, "I'm forever filling these damn boxes up." He could not blame me, I never smoked.

Mrs. Pearce (Olive Sainsbury) was quite attractive and good looking, but her language was disgusting, and she couldn't care less who heard her.

I remember one morning we were cycling to go to work there, and just before the railway bridge there was a car down in the brook. When we got to the Chase we found out about it: the night before it was the Hunt Ball at Broadway, and Philip Chandler from Campden was bringing Mrs. Pearce back from the Ball. They were both drunk, and apparently neither of them was hurt.

After spending all that money on the property, they only stayed about two years. Some years later, Jimmy Pearce was killed in a fall during a race in India.

Not long after the work at Charingworth was completed, Mrs. Pearce senior bought a farm at Blackwell for her younger son, Teddy. Again Pyments had the contract to carry out the alterations to the house and buildings. This was a much longer distance to cycle night and morning, so I bought a second-hand motor-bike off Escott Elsley. It was a large, long, square-tank Sunbeam. I told them at work I should be arriving on a motor-bike the next morning. Ernest Buckland ("Peony") was working with us at the time, so I told him I could take him on the pillion. When we arrived there, the foreman, who was old Charlie ("Waggy") Withers from Blockley, said "What make did you say it was?" I said, "A Sunbeam." He said, "It sounded to me like a bloody thunderstorm."

There was quite a nice looking girl in the village, Georgina Cox. She used to be waiting along the road when we were coming home in the evenings. I went back over to see her a few times, and after the job there was complete she wrote a couple of letters, but I never answered them. Then about 3 or 4 years ago Charlie Nicholls and his wife went to Newbold-on-Stour, and during a conversation with some ladies there mentioned they came from Campden, and one of the ladies said, "Do you know Fred Coldicott?" Of course they said yes, they did. She said, "Please remember me to him, I was Georgina Cox, and have never forgotten him." That was over fifty years later.

In July 1930 Uncle Bob, Dad's younger brother, died aged 58 years. He was a Boer War veteran, and I always maintain that the terrible illness he had in South Africa was the main cause of his death. Every year he seemed to have an attack of malaria.

Another Campden character who died not long before Uncle Bob was "Slap", Charlie Blakeman. I think he was sixty-nine. I can picture him now, with his old black bowler hat, breeches and leggings, staggering up Sheep Street on his way home from the pub. He had a well-deserved reputation for being what my Father always said was "the craftiest man he ever knew".

On one occasion I was sent with Joey James to do some roof repairs at Campden House when the Hon. Charles Noel lived there. At lunch time a maid came out with a jug of tea for us. She was a very nice girl, but we had difficulty understanding her very strong Scottish accent. Anyway, I chatted her up, and arranged to meet her the following Saturday afternoon at the end of the drive in Dyers Lane. When I rode up on the old Sunbeam she was out there waiting. I said, "Get on the pillion", which she did. I hadn't bothered to put the bike out of gear, but was just holding the clutch lever up in my hand. I turned around to say was she alright, and my hand slipped off the clutch lever. The motor-bike leapt forward. Off we both came, and thank heaven neither of us was hurt, but "Janet's" skirt was split open all down the front. The motor-bike was not damaged, but she was a bit dubious about getting on it again (I don't blame her). Anyway, I took her home and Mother did some repairs on her skirt. We eventually went to Evesham and went to the cinema. I took her out a few more times, but she was getting too serious, really, so I broke it off.

The St. James Club soon came to an end when the Rev. Badger left Campden, so when the darker evenings came, unless you were a drinker and went to the pubs, there was nowhere to go. I sent away for a punch-ball and a set of boxing gloves. At home there was a large attic room which was not furnished, so I fixed up the punch ball and told any of the lads who wanted to, could come whenever they liked. Charlie Stanley, Oswald Stanley, Val Hobbs, Bob Parsons from Berrington Mill - they came regularly, and several others would come occasionally. George ("Lucas") Greenall came quite a lot, but he very rarely put the gloves on and had a go. Mother used to come up and sit and watch us; she loved it.

At this time George Plested, who had married Alice Hughes, was living in the house where George Badham used to live, and up the passage, at the rear, was a large shed that had been Mr. Badham's workshop. Myself, Val Hobbs and Ray Crump decided to start a club, and George Plested said he would let us have the old workshop. I took my punchball along and fixed it up, we obtained a dartboard, tennis table, and various games like draughts, cards, etc. Altogether, about twenty joined us. We charged them twopence a week, and for quite a long period it was a great success. It must have been two years, then several of us, including me, Val Hobbs, Wilf Plested, etc., started courting. The

55

younger ones wouldn't take on the responsibility of running it, so unfortunately it gradually petered out.

The gearbox on my motor-bike had gradually packed up. In the end I could only use top gear, which meant I had to run with it and then jump on, and couldn't slow down much around corners. One day on the sharp bend where you turn down to Compton Scorpion on the Shipston Road I had to go so fast I didn't make it, and ran across the grass verge into the hedge. I wasn't hurt except for a few scratches, but after that I sold the old bike for scrap. Mother was very relieved, because she was always worried when I was out on it.

Work in the building trade around here was very slack and getting much more competitive; firms were beginning to look for work over a larger area than ever before. Pyments had a contract to build a house at Minchinhampton, over forty miles away from Campden. Michael Grove was the foreman in charge; it was too far to travel backwards and forwards, then, so it meant lodging there.

They also had a contract to modernise and overhaul St. Edward's Hall in Stow-on-the-Wold. We were there about three months, cycling there and back every day. We were allowed half an hour cycling time in the mornings, but of course we had to cycle home in our own time.

I shall never forget one evening six or seven of us were cycling home. It had been a blistering hot day. When we got to the hill between the turning for Upper Swell and the Coach and Horses at Ganborough we all got off to walk up. We could see a dirty old tramp coming down the hill towards us; when he was fifty or sixty yards from us, he stopped suddenly, put his nose up in the air, then clapped his hands over his face and hurried down towards us and shouted "There's poison gas, be careful." When he got to us we could see it was poor old "Woffler" Blake. He was a Campden man who had lived at the bottom of Poppet's Alley with his wife and daughter. His wife left him, taking the little girl with her, and Woffler just let himself go and became a "milestone inspector"; in other words, took to the road.

Anyway, as we continued up the hill there was the most horrible smell. When we investigated, someone had dumped a whole heap of rotten fish behind some bushes. But I shall never forget the look on old Woffler's face, and the way he sniffed with his head up in the air.

When the Stow-on-the-Wold contract was completed, Arthur Watkinson had finalised his plan to construct two swimming baths in what had been the Recreation Ground between Catbrook and Broad Campden [not to be confused with the Campden bathing lake, built by

56

the Guild of Handicraft in 1903 and approached through Bessie Keen and Westington Mill; see page 35 above] one quite large one for adults, and a smaller one for youngsters. Every bit of earth was dug out by hand, most of it wheeled in barrows and levelled out around the sides, and a lot of the sub-soil taken in lorries and dumped. It was lovely hot weather at the time; I remember we looked like African natives. Mr. Watkinson himself strutted around every day in swimming trunks: he put me in mind of a large pot-bellied Zulu chief. When the actual building started, he put quite a few silver coins in the concrete base, and when he came in the mornings, he would put silver coins in the brickwork, making sure that by putting them in during the morning there were several courses of bricks over them before evening. The water supply came from two springs which started near Adelaide Coppice. They were collected and piped to a filter bed containing graduated layers of clinkers, then into the baths. There was a valve where it could be shut off and diverted into the ditch. There were about ten changing cubicles in the adult bath, and one for boys and one for girls in the children's; both baths were surrounded by a seven feet high fence. The baths proved to be very popular, people coming from a very wide area. If the weather was decent, there were crowds came at week-ends from as far away as Birmingham, Coventry and Worcester.

One of the features of Campden Grammar School was their Cadet Corps. They always had a good bugle band, and frequently, much to the delight of the residents, they would come marching through the streets in their uniforms. But unfortunately, in 1931 the Government decided they would no longer give them a support grant, so that was the end of another old custom. Everyone in Campden was very sad about it.

In the summer of 1931 our old schoolmaster, Mr. G. W. Dewey, died aged 67 years. I think he had been headmaster here for twenty years. He was definitely a hard man when it came to doling out punishment, but he was dedicated to his job, for sure. Speaking for myself, I'm sure I had more than my share of the cane, but I am also sure, on hindsight, it did me more good than harm. One thing I always admired him for - he was a great patriot, and he taught us to be patriotic, but he never once tried to impress any political views on us.

At this time the building and construction firms in this area were having a very tough time, and one day Harold Pyment came round on his bicycle and told everyone to report at the office at ten o'clock the following morning. We were all gathered in the basement outside the office as instructed, when Harold and Arthur came out. They told us the exact situation, which was that they hadn't got a single job on the books, but they had been in touch with Mr. Wells at the Unemployment Office at Moreton-in-Marsh, and explained to him that they weren't sacking anyone, but laying the men off temporarily until work started up again. So this meant you could draw dole money and have your card stamped. I wasn't very keen on signing on the dole, and in any case, being single, I would only have about eleven shillings per week. So that evening I saw George ("Lucas") Greenall, who I knew was out of work, and we arranged to cycle down to Joe Webb's at Mickleton, and try and get a job on his market garden. Down we went next morning (Friday), saw Mr. Webb at his house. After quite a talk to him about Campden, he told us where to go to find his foreman, Mr. Arthur Brain, and to tell him on Mr. Webb's instructions we could start work on the Monday morning. "Art" Brain told us to report to Mr. Harry Seward at the Lower Field, seven o'clock on the Monday morning.

When we arrived there, we joined four other men, and we were all issued with a spade. The field had been planted with fruit trees and had recently been ploughed, but of course they could not get too near the trees with the tractor, so about five feet wide down the rows of trees had to be dug by hand. One of the regular men was a tall, ginger-haired fellow, and I heard him say to his mates, "Get stuck in, we'll show these two from Campden how to do a bit of digging." So I said to Lucas, "Keep up with me, they are going to try and show us up." Well, it was just the reverse, we were just ahead of them when it came to lunchtime at one o'clock.

During the hour at lunchtime, we all chatted together and became good friends. Those four were Bob Roberts (the ginger-haired one), Tom ("York") Hands from Willersey, Harry Debereux from Mickleton, and Bill Brighton from Saintbury. Bill only had one eye, but he was considered to be the best football goalkeeper for miles around. He played for Badsey Rangers when they were one of the finest amateur teams in the country. Harry Debereux (we called him "Debbie") was a man after my own heart: he always brought a ferret and some nets to work, if there were any rabbits in the vicinity.

Joseph Webb was a very staunch Chapel man, and before he lived at Mickleton he kept the bakery shop in Campden where Mr. Tom Heritage was, and is now carried on by the Gabb family.* I wouldn't know the exact figures, but I am sure he employed between twenty and thirty men, and probably as many women, because he had several acres of

---

* *See page 6 above. The bakery as a business has since been sold.*

58

glasshouses. His foreman, or manager, was Art Brain, also a very strict Chapel man. His nickname to the men was "Ferret". It was remarkable how he could creep up on you without you realising he was around; if you were working in the middle of a field, he would appear behind you almost as though he had dropped from the sky. It was very uncanny.

After about seven weeks there was a note from Pyments to say things had improved, and I could start back with them again if I wished. The next morning I went and saw Mr. Brain and explained the situation to him, and arranged with him to have my cards at the end of the week so that I could start back at Pyments on the Monday morning. When I went to the office at the week-end for my cards and money old Ferret shook hands with me, wished me luck, and said there would always be a job for me if the occasion arose. Fortunately it never did, for the take-home pay was only 29 shillings and threepence a week. I must say, I enjoyed my few weeks at Mickleton; they were a grand lot of fellows.

I remember the 1931-1932 football season very well. Campden had the best football team they had ever had (that's my opinion), and every home game was well supported. The climax came in January, when they travelled to Bourton-on-the-Water and easily beat Bourton Rovers to win the Bourton Hospital Cup. There were over three hundred supporters travelled to Bourton-on-the-Water that day.

When I started back at Pyments on the Monday I was sent with several others to Blockley, where they had two fairly large alteration jobs. The one I went to was for Mrs. Whale at Porch House. She was a very kind, elderly lady who kept us well supplied with tea.

After several weeks at Blockley I went to Broadway, where they had quite a large contract at a large house facing the Green; it is now Harrison's Garage. Charlie Withers senior was foreman on the jobs at Blackwell and Stow-on-the-Wold. He was alright if there was no pub near. If he could get to a pub during lunch hour he was always the worse for drink in the afternoon. One day at the Broadway job Mr. Harold Pyment appeared at two o'clock; he hung around until nearly three o'clock, when old "Waggy" Withers came back, his old face like the rising sun. Anyway, Harold told him if he couldn't be there to carry on work at two o'clock, how could he expect the men to, and he sacked him on the spot.

About this time I remember there was a serious farm fire at Briar Hill Farm, Broad Campden. Leonard Levi Potter was the tenant farmer at the time. I think the damage was estimated to be over £2,000.

I must write a few words about Charlie Veale, who died a few weeks after Potter's farm fire. He had worked as carter for the Haydon family for over forty years, and if there is any reward for living a good life, then I'm sure he will qualify. He was a genuine, hard-working, honest man, who I should think never said a cross word to anyone in his life - although he had good cause to, for his wife was the complete opposite: not too clean, scruffily dressed, and spent most of her time at the jug and bottle lid-holes at the pubs. Mr. Veale played in the Town Band for most of his life, and was well loved by everybody. It was a pleasure to know such a man. He was seventy-three when he died, and had worked up till three or four weeks before he died.

Down at Butcher Jack Coldicott's barns in the Calfs House field there was a bean rick, and anyone who walked by could see the rats running about, so one weekend it was decided to have a ratting party. They took four good terriers and dismantled the bean rick. In about three hours they had killed three hundred and eighty nine fully grown rats. The next morning another five were found and killed, which made to a total of three hundred and ninety four.

After Jim Gibbs who lived at Mary's Acre died, Pyments had quite a lot of work at the farm buildings next to the Baker's Arms at Broad Campden. The large barn was converted into a house and some of the cow stalls were also made into a house. There was a considerable amount of modernising done at Mary's Acre also. Gibbs' barn was the third lovely old barn to be turned into a house. The other two, Izod's Barn and High Barn, were converted about 1926 by Mr. Blair-Fish and his partner, Mr. Budgen, who lived at the Malt House.

Whilst we were working at Broad Campden old "Sykes", Charles Seitz, died. He was seventy-seven years old. They found him dead at the foot of the staircase in the cottage where he lived, next to the Quaker Chapel. What a tragedy his life had been: once a handsome, well-educated young man who came from a wealthy and good family, to live most of his life as a cattle drover. He had a brother, Fred, who was a chemist in Liverpool, and a sister who came to Campden once and stayed for a while with Mr. Henry Haydon, the farmer. During my memories of him he was always quite harmless, but my father and others said that when he was a younger man he occasionally got drunk and boisterous. On one occasion, at Stratford-on-Avon, he got away from three policemen. When he came up in front of Canon Bourne on another occasion, at Campden court, Canon Bourne said, "I'm going to send you to prison for a week." Sykes said, "You can't do that, Bourne, I've got a hen sitting at home." He always attended any "fêtes" etc. in Campden and the villages around; they all knew him well, and always gave him a cup of tea and some food. *

About the same time that Sykes died, there was another old Campden personality died - Mrs. Annie Green, aged seventy-one years. Before her marriage she was a member of the Tombs family, well-known throughout the district as stonemasons and builders. Annie Green, for nearly forty years, was the local midwife. I know she brought my brother and myself into the world. Mother was very friendly with her and often visited her. She had one son named Bert who went to Canada about 1922, but returned to Campden just before his mother died. He eventually got married and lived at Ebrington. Mrs. Green was a very popular and well-respected woman.

What is now a grocery store next to the Red Lion Inn was then two houses. In the one next to the pub lived Annie Green, and the other one was a boot and shoe repair shop kept by Joe Hands and his wife. He was good at his trade, and quite a lot of people had their footwear made by him. He was quite a cheerful man, despite the fact that he was stone deaf. If you wanted to tell him anything, you had to write it down on a slate. Many times when I was a schoolboy I have sat in his workshop watching him at work. I don't know why, but he always called me "Johnny".

In March 1933 there was another suicide in Campden - Robert James Dickinson, living with his wife Elizabeth in Cider Mill Lane. His wife, who had been out to work, came back home to find him dead, hanging from the stair bannister with a piece of rope. He was sixty-eight years old. He and his wife came to Campden nearly forty years before as licensed pedlars; he used to say they came originally from Nottingham. He was quite a small man who could neither read nor write, but he had been the local agent for the "News of the World", and for many years he had delivered the paper around Campden, Broad Campden and Blockley

* *Graham Greene's "Reflections", published by Reinhardt Books in 1990, contains an account of Charlie Seitz's life and death which originally appeared in the "Spectator" magazine in 1933. Though Graham Greene was living in Campden at the time, according to Mr. Coldicott his article contains at least two significant errors of fact. Greene says that Seitz, "born in the blaze and glare" of India, "died frozen...in a Cotswold cottage on a bed of straw." According to Mr. Coldicott, who has confirmed it with Val Hobbs, Seitz was found (as he says above) at the bottom of his stairs with a broken neck. Greene also says that Seitz walked to Evesham several times each week, "eight miles each way by road, but he did not go by road. He knew every gap in every hedge for miles around..." In fact, according to Mr. Coldicott, Seitz never the left the main road and would go a long way around in order to stay on the road. Indeed, Seitz had a saying: "The hard road for the old man."*

61

every Sunday. He attained "notoriety" by stopping King Edward VII's car in Broad Campden and selling him a copy of the "News of the World". After that, the proprietors of the newspaper gave him a brass plate, which was attached to his paper-selling bag, on which was inscribed the Royal Coat of Arms.

"Liz" Dickinson was a very nasty and disagreeable person. She had been up before the magistrates several times for insulting and assaulting people.

On the Saturday evening of Scuttlebrook Wake day 1933 it poured down with rain, and continued all night. Early on the Sunday morning the huge horse-chestnut tree near the pump, without any warning, came crashing down, part of it falling across "Buller" Atwell's caravan which was parked outside Wixey's Grocery Shop. Miraculously no one was hurt, but naturally very shocked. I know Mr. Atwell tried to get some compensation, but none of the local councils would accept responsibility.

I can well remember Christmas Day 1933, because on that day another well-known and very much respected old Campden man died: Richard Dunn, seventy-nine years old. He was another who I could almost guarantee had never done anything wrong, or said a bad word about anyone in his life. For many years he was secretary to the Stroud Benefit Society. His wife had been Miss Haines, sister to old "Bummer" Haines, the plumber. Mr. and Mrs. Dunn were great friends of my parents, and Mother often went up to have a chat with Mrs. Dunn. I think they went to school together*.

By this time the building trade had considerably improved, and Pyments were really quite busy, and as well as Campden and Broad Campden men they had five on regularly from Blockley. The lorry driver was Bert Andrews from Stretton-on-Fosse. Unfortunately for Bert he became ill, so Mr. Arthur Pyment came to me and said he would have to drive the lorry and he would want me to go with him to load and unload. One day he left the lorry in the yard and walked up Sheep Street to his bungalow for lunch. At two o'clock he hadn't turned up, so I thought, "To save him walking down I'll drive the lorry up to his drive." When he came down his drive, I was sat in the passenger seat. He said, "Who drove this lorry up here?" I said, "I did." So he said, "Why the devil

---

* *Martha Dunn was the Infant School teacher when the Ashbees arrived in Campden. She figures prominently in the Guild of Handicraft's story as one of those (relatively few) local people who actively welcomed the Guild. She corresponded regularly with the Ashbees after they left Campden.*

didn't you say you could drive. Here am I wasting my time, will you take the job on?" I said I would until Bert Andrews came back. Anyway, it went on week after week, until one day they said would I take it on permanently. I said I would if they increased my pay by two pence per hour. They agreed, so I became permanent lorry driver.

The lorry at that time was only a 30 cwt. Morris Commercial, and when they were busy it was difficult to keep the jobs supplied with materials, so I recommended that a larger lorry would cut down the journeys by half. They were good bosses and realised I was right, and soon a new Bedford three tonner arrived.

There were very few building materials delivered then. All the sand came from Alfred Longford's farm at Stretton-on-Fosse. You had to go to the farmhouse to get the key to the gate of the sand-pit, then you had to dig and load up your lorry yourself, lock the gate again and return the key, where old "Alfie" Longford would see how much you had. If he wasn't available, Mr. Harris the cowman was supposed to look. Stone chippings, used for concrete, I fetched from the Holt Quarry on the Northwick Estate, halfway between Blockley and the Oxford Road. Mr. Brooks from Blockley was in charge there; he was the grandfather of Bob Brooks, the present builder in Campden. Bricks and rooftiles came from Captain Spencer-Churchill's works at Blockley Railway Station. All the work at the brickyard was, "except those working in the clay pit", piece work, so the bigger the production, the bigger the wages.

I well remember one day I had driven the lorry in front of the kiln entrance, and whilst the men were loading it, I sat in the empty kiln next to it reading the paper. It was a bitterly cold day, and it was lovely and warm in the kiln. Anyway, all of a sudden in walked Capt. Churchill, Jack Hull the manager, and Bill Webb the yard foreman. Captain Churchill took one look at me, turned to Jack Hull and said, "Who's that man? Sack him immediately."

Occasionally I fetched brick or land-drain pipe from the Honeybourne Brick and Pipe Works. The owner, who lived in the house there, was Mr. Tomlinson. His only child, a son, was killed in the Great War. I liked going there because Mr. Tomlinson always came out from the office and gave me two shillings.

Most of the stone I fetched from either the Fish Quarry at the top of Broadway Hill, or from the quarry at the top of Stanway Hill called Coscombe Quarry. Occasionally I had to go to Jackdaw Quarry - that is in the Five Mile Drive, going in from the entrance on the Blockley to Broad Campden Road near Hangman's Hall. All quoins, mullioned windows, and fireplaces I fetched from Farmington Quarries on the Bourton-on-the-Water to Northleach Road.

In March 1934 another old Campdonian died: Richard Withers the blacksmith, aged 82 years. With his son, Charlie, they kept the smithy and horse-shoeing shop in the middle of Church Cottages near the Church. Both father and son were very friendly and jolly and never seemed to mind when we were schoolboys standing and watching them working. I remember them telling us the business had been there in their family over two hundred years, and at one time there had been a saw-pit on the premises, where all the timber used on the Campden Estate was cut up. Richard and Charlie were both bellringers for most of their adult lives, and Richard's nephew Harry was sexton at the Church for many years.

Only five months after the death of his father, Charles William Withers died, aged fifty-six years. It came as a shock to all the inhabitants of Campden, for he seemed such a strong, healthy man who never had an illness. Unfortunately he was a bachelor, and the last to carry on the family trade. Every day for as long as I could remember, at exactly ten o'clock in the morning, he would take his bread and cheese down to the Eight Bells, have just one pint of beer, and straight back to work; he never even took his leather apron off. As far as I know his only hobby was bell ringing. He had been a regular bell-ringer for thirty-six years.

In 1933 Mr. Jimmy Strange purchased Westington Quarries and brought his family - wife and two sons - from Defford near Pershore to live in Campden. He was an engineer by profession, and originated from Warrington in Lancashire. It was not long before he installed his own electricity supply, which powered several types of stone saws and drills. When he came to Campden he brought with him from Defford Charles Wright and his family. Charles was in charge of stone sawing. He was a good, hard-working, honest fellow. I was in the fire service with him for a good many years. I remember he always brought a jar of pea-shell wine over to the fire station at Christmas time.

As soon as the quarries became operational after Mr. Strange took them over Pyments had their stone from there, including all quoins, windows, fireplaces, etc. Down the mine itself he had loads of horse manure and soil taken, where he grew mushrooms very successfully. Down there the temperature did not vary much, which was ideal.

In 1934 Campden Town Band and Blockley Sports Club were short of funds. They joined forces, formed a committee, and decided to promote a boxing tournament to raise funds. Myself, Val Hobbs and Lew Morgan were invited to help. Lew Morgan had experience as a masseur and boxer's second when he lived in south Wales; he was trainer for Campden Town Football Club for a number of years. To save expenses it was decided to hold the event in Haydon's barn near the Church. A ring was obtained from Evesham for a very small fee, and Mr. Raynor Booth from Mickleton agreed to referee. He had been a heavyweight member of the Cambridge University Boxing Team, and had gained his "blue".

The contests were arranged: some from Blockley, and some of us from Campden. The barn was absolutely packed out with spectators; of course it was something completely new for Campden. Because of my size and weight I had been matched with someone named Chownes, but unfortunately when the bus arrived he had failed to turn up, so I just acted as a second in one corner. It turned out to be quite a success. The contest between Val Hobbs and Bob "Rusty" Merriman was a real thriller, the referee at the end having to give a draw.

A few weeks later, a few from Blockley came over and we took them up to Gladwin's barn at Westington for an evening's sparring. A soldier named Hawtin, on leave from the Grenadier Guards, came with the Blockley lads. He said he was his battalion heavyweight champion. I was the only one near his weight, so I agreed to spar with him. It soon developed into a real scrap (much to the delight of the others). Anyway, in the end he was glad to pack it in, we shook hands, and finished up good friends. I thought he was a very nice chap.

Soon after I took on the lorry driver's job, I bought a four-ten folding cartridge gun from George ("Spo") Spiers (he was a real old poacher). When folded, you could carry it under your coat without anyone knowing, but the reason I bought it was to carry in the lorry cab with me. I was never short of a rabbit in those days, and during the game season I usually had a pheasant or two every week. Pyments had the contract to build a new house at Temple Guiting; I had a regular supply of pheasants whilst that job was on, they were so plentiful in that area. Looking back in hindsight, it was a marvel I was never caught. I certainly was very lucky.

Pyments did quite a lot of ecclesiastical work in the carpentry shop, and occasionally it meant I had longer journeys. One of the first was to take an oak lectern to a church at Brentwood in Essex. Bert Wilkes, who was out of work at the time, came with me for a ride, and on the way back I made a little detour and called at Hemel Hempstead to see my brother. He had a pleasant surprise when he saw me and Bert.

65

On the top floor of the Guild Workshop, over Hart's silversmith's shop, Mr. Alec Miller the sculptor had his studio. I often used to go up and watch him at work, and sometimes if it was a large figure he was working on he would mark a piece with chalk, give me a mallet and chisel, and say "There, you can take that off for me". I always got on well with Alec Miller. He was a very nice man; the only thing I did not like was his politics - they were extreme left. On one occasion when he visited Russia he brought me back a small wooden carving of a Russian peasant ploughing with a horse.

On two occasions I took him and his carvings to the Royal Academy at Burlington House in London. The first time we stopped in Oxford, and he took me into his son Alastair's rooms in Christ Church College for breakfast. I was glad I had my breakfast before I left home: they had strong tea, no milk, just a slice of lemon in it; with a struggle I did manage to drink it. The following year Mr. Miller entered a large sculpture of the Sphinx. If I remember right, it was carved from a French stone called "salamander". This time we took Michael Grove with us, because it was much too heavy for one man to lift. When me and Mike Grove were carrying it in to Burlington House, there was a whole battery of press photographers taking our photographs. Naturally we were quite expecting to see ourselves in some of the next day's newspapers, but it wasn't in any of them; but a few weeks afterwards Alec Miller showed us the photo in a foreign newspaper called the "Straits Times". The very first journey I made to London for Mr. Miller was to take a memorial stone to a very quaint little old church, right in the centre of London - all I can remember is, it was near Threadneedle Street where the Bank of England is.

Another good trip was to Formby in Lancashire. Alec Miller had been commissioned to make a life-sized sculpture of "Our Lord" being crucified for a Roman Catholic church and convent at Formby. When it was completed it really was a marvellous piece of work. The cross, I remember, was fourteen feet high. The arrangements were made for Pyments to take it and erect it in the grounds of the convent. The materials for concrete would be on the site, and we would sleep at the convent for the night. Michael Grove came with me, and we had a good journey there, arriving much sooner than I expected, so we got cracking and by about half past five we had got it propped in position and concreted in. The nuns were ever so good. They gave us a jolly good tea, and we were in Southport, the seaside resort, before seven o'clock. Mike was a very good companion. Like me he wasn't a "drinker".

There was a fortune teller on the sea-front. Mike went in and had his fortune told, and seemed very impressed when he came out, but he would never divulge what she told him. A few years ago, not long before he died, I referred to the occasion, and he told me it was uncanny - everything that fortune teller had told him came true.

There had been a lot of publicity in the Press about the Mersey Tunnel, which had not been opened all that long. I was determined to go through it as we came back through Birkenhead and Liverpool. I still have the toll ticket now.

In those days, every year the Army Southern Command held their military tattoo at Tidworth on Salisbury Plain, and the Great Western Railway used to run an excursion train to it. It was a magnificent spectacle, and I went on two occasions. The second time I was very lucky to make it. The train left Campden Station at four o'clock. Pyments were very busy at the time, and I said I would work as long as possible, allowing myself time to get to the station. Early in the afternoon I was returning from Northwick Brickyard with a load of bricks for a bungalow in Blind Lane, Westington. When I got to the Tiltapin Corner at the top of Sheep Street, around the corner, going like merry hell on his wrong side came Cyril Harris driving in Callaway's baker's van. We met head on, the front of my lorry was bashed in, and the front axle broken. Poor old Cyril's van was like a concertina, and the back door had fled open and the bread and cakes all over the road. The miracle was, apart from being badly shaken, neither of us was hurt. I ran down the road to Pyments' office. They rang up the police, and when Sergeant Tombs came up he carried on to Cyril for being on the wrong side of the road. No doubt we were both going too fast, because like me Cyril was hurrying to get his round finished so that he could catch the train.

The last time I saw Cyril I was sat on the side of the road near a village called Witmarsum in north Holland watching a battery of artillery go by, when someone shouted "Colonel" (my Army nickname). It was Cyril, waving from the cab of one of the G.T.V.'s (Gun Towing Vehicles). Not long afterwards, going into a field, the vehicle he was in was blown up by a German mine, and poor Cyril was killed. A good lad, just the opposite to "Goggles", his brother.

In 1934 I was best man at my brother's wedding at Hemel Hempstead. He married Edna Mortimer, the only daughter of Tom Mortimer, manager and part owner of the Hemel Hempstead Brick Company; her only brother Dennis was until recently chairman of Luton Town Football Club. My mother, Aunty Lil (Uncle Bob's wife), and myself of course went. We hired Jack Horne to take us; it was a lovely wedding, and we all enjoyed ourselves. I got on well with one of Edna's pals, a lovely girl named Betty Williams. She begged me to write to her, but I never did. Two or three years later she got married, and died soon afterwards.

In the Spring of 1936 I joined the fire brigade. Ormonde Plested was captain, but he retired and Bert Cooke was made captain. We had a hand-cart, a stand-pipe and half a dozen hoses; these were kept in a shed at "Stale" Benfield's in Sheep Street. We met once a month, and our retaining fee was £1, paid at Christmas. We had one ladder, which was kept in the Market Hall.

I am over-running my story a little, because on February the ninth 1935 I was married at Campden Roman Catholic Church to Millicent Mary Clifton who originated from Exton in the County of Rutland, which was the smallest county in England, but has now been taken into Leicestershire. I consented to a Roman Catholic ceremony because I don't believe in arguing about religion. I got the impression Mother wasn't altogether happy about it, but she never actually said so. Bill came from Hemel Hempstead to be my best man; I only wish my Dad could have been there.

Millie's father had been head gardener for the Earls of Gainsborough at Exton Hall, and when the Hon. Charles Noel came to live at Campden House Mr. and Mrs. Clifton came with him.

I first saw Millie in 1933. We were working in Campden Town Hall. I came out of there to go to Pyments' yard in Sheep Street, and this young lady was walking along by the Noel Arms. As she looked at me I gave her a saucy wink; she smiled, but carried on. I looked out for her but never saw her again until about twelve months later: I was driving the lorry across the Leasows, having taken some materials to "Tally Ho" where Alec Miller lived, when who should be coming across the footpath was this same young lady who I had briefly seen a year earlier. Of course I arranged it so that I arrived at the gate at the same time as she did. She told me she had been spending a few days with her parents at Campden House, but was returning that day to Exton. A few weeks later I was in Evesham, and I met her again coming out of a shop. She told me her father had retired, and they were now living in Honeybourne. She had terminated her job at Exton, and had come home to her parents at Honeybourne. I made a date to go to Honeybourne on the following Monday evening. Well, my luck was right out, we had two days of snow blizzards and all the roads were impassable. After about a week the roads were beginning to improve, so I walked to Honeybourne, spent a couple of hours there, and walked back home. Her parents were ever such nice people, and made me very welcome. A short while after, Millie came to Campden to work at Miss

Hargreave's Hotel and Tearooms, called the "Golden Cockerel". She worked there until we got married. Millie had one older sister named Rose, and one brother, Charlie, who was also older. I got on well with Charlie; he was a nice fellow with a great sense of humour. We slept at Honeybourne on our wedding night, and four times during the night alarm clocks woke us up. Charlie had borrowed them, set them to go off at different times, and hidden them away in the drawers and wardrobe.

At this time Harold Pyment, who had been living at Midland Bank House, moved out to live where Joe Hands and Annie Green had lived; he had made the two houses into one. Arthur Pyment, who was a great friend of Mr. Homer the Midland Bank manager, asked him if I could take over the tenancy, which I did, and at a reduced rent. Harold Pyment had been paying 12/6 per week, and I paid 10/-, so I was very lucky, because of course it was just across the road from my mother.

In June of 1936 old Edward Rimell died. He was Campden's oldest male inhabitant. Everyone knew him as "Ned". He was a very familiar figure in Campden, riding his old tricycle. He was a distant relative of my father's. My great grandmother was a Miss Rimell; she was a sister of William Rimell who lived at Berrington Court. Ned Rimell in his younger days was a very popular amateur jockey. Ned lived at the "Barley Mow", and when we were lads, we always went and wished him a happy New Year, and each one always had a sixpence.

About this time I experienced one of the worst journeys I have ever had. Sir Stafford Cripps was living at Filkins, a fairly large village near Fairford. He had built a row of cottages, something like almshouses, and Pyments had been given the contract to make and deliver all the front doors and frames, to be made in Norfolk Oak. The cottages had to be opened on a given date by a Cabinet colleague of Sir Stafford's, Mr. George Lansbury. Not long before the opening day a very severe wintery spell of weather set in. It snowed for several days on and off, and everybody on the building work were temporarily put off. One day, after I had been at home a few days, Harold Pyment came to see me. He said they were in a panic at Filkins: the opening ceremony was getting close, and it was essential that they had the oak doors and frames immediately. Mr. Pyment said, "I'm not ordering you to go, Fred", but would I try to get through to Filkins the next day. Well, what was I to do, I was never one to shirk a challenge, so I said I would "have a go".

Millie made me two thermos flasks of tea, plenty of sandwiches, and off I went the following morning. For long stretches the roads were

69

single track, with the snow piled each side anything between two feet and six feet high. The worst part was from the Rissington turn to Burford; fortunately I never met anything between Stow and Burford. If I had, someone would have had to reverse a hell of a long way. Down the hill going into Burford I did the last fifty yards sideways. From the top of Burford to Filkins there seemed to be less snow, but still very hazardous. Anyway, I made it. The foreman on the housing site said how pleased he was, and gave me £1. It was a great relief to Millie when I walked in home at tea-time, she had been worried sick all day.

About twenty minutes to midnight on May 5th my daughter Betty was born at home. I was sat on the stairs listening; Nurse Groom, a stern Victorian type was in attendance. Some time after, when she came downstairs - I was sat in the kitchen - she told me I had a lovely little daughter and I could pop upstairs to see them, but only for a minute or two. When I returned to the kitchen we sat and had a cup of tea. In a nice way I suggested that if the birth was registered half an hour later, that as a regular reader of the "Daily Mail" I would be eligible for £5 and a new perambulator, as May 6th was, of course, King George V's Jubilee day. I'm afraid old Nurse Groom was disgusted; anyway, I tried.

Campden had organised a large celebration programme for the Jubilee, and all children under fourteen years of age were entitled to a celebration mug. I went up to Guy Pemberton's house in the morning and told him I had come for a mug. Naturally, he said "You have no children", so when I told him I was a proud father, he was quite thrilled and made me go in and celebrate with a drink along with him and his wife. In the parade for the best decorated vehicles I drove Pyments' lorry, and we had first prize. During the afternoon in the Recreation Ground I captained a tug-of-war team, and we won first prize, each member of the team receiving a cigarette case with a Jubilee medal on it; I still have it now.

In June 1936 a new Vicar was inducted. He was the Rev. Bryan O'Loughlin, an Irishman who started off by studying to be a Roman Catholic priest, but half way through his studies he decided he was on the wrong track, and became a Protestant parson. He became quite a popular vicar, along with his wife and two daughters. After being here a few years he was made Canon O'Loughlin.

Not long after I was demobbed from the Army I was working with Wilson Bennett and Jack Bruce repairing the stonework around some of the windows in the church. We were sat having our lunch one day, and the Rev. O'Loughlin was talking to us. When Wilson Bennett asked him if he had ever seen or heard anything "spooky" in the church, "Yes," said the Vicar, "On several occasions I have seen the figure of a man in a monk's habit cross over in front of the altar, from where the vestry is to the Gainsborough Chapel." There was no doubt he was convinced he had seen the apparition.

Two or three weeks after Christmas 1936 Mrs. Charlotte Chamberlain died. She was the wife of Mr. W.C. Chamberlain, who ran a printing business and stationery shop at Kelmscott House. She was a very well-liked and active lady in the social activities of the town. She was a good actress, and always took part in the Amateur Dramatic Society's productions. She was also one of the founder members of the Women's Institute. Her daughter May was about my age, and they had two older sons, Wolford and Collett. Wolford was a very good footballer and played on the right wing for Campden Town Club for several seasons.

Pyments had a contract to make and fit all-new pews in Abington Church, Northampton. When they had made them in the workshops, I had to transport them to Northampton in the lorry. On the Monday morning I took Bill Wall, Arthur Bunting, and Ernie Lockyer with me. They lodged there for the week, and I would fetch them back for the week-end. The second Monday I took Mike Grove as well, and I stayed all day helping so that I could bring Mike back home. Well, we had a terrible journey back. It started snowing at tea-time, the windscreen wipers on the lorry packed up, and I had to drive with my side window down with my head half way out to see the road. The lorry headlights weren't very good, and having to drive with the window down, we were both cold and miserable. I remember I had to brake suddenly at Daventry Cross Roads, the lorry skidded, and we ended up facing the opposite way. I shall never forget old Mike's words when we eventually arrived home. He said, "There I went through the Great War, but I was never so scared as I have been tonight." All I can say is, thank God he was with me.

One day I was taking some materials and Arthur Pyment said, "I will come with you, Fred, and see how the job is going on." On the return journey we were coming between Banbury and Brailes when I suddenly pulled up. Mr. Pyment said, "What the devil is the matter". I said, "I've just seen an Ancient Briton". I reversed back and there he was in the field, just as you would imagine an Ancient Briton would look like. We found out afterwards it was Theodore Lamb who lived in a dug-out in the field, which was on his brother's farm. They say he had been "crossed in love" when he was a young man. After I had been demobbed in 1946 I took Millie, my wife, to see him. He came out into

71

the road, so I got out of the car with my camera. He said "You are not taking my photo until you have given me two shillings", so I gave him the two shillings and took his photo, which I have now got in my scrapbook.

The week beginning Monday the seventh of December, 1936, was a dramatic week in the history of our country. The whole of the population were anxiously listening to every news bulletin on the radio wondering what was going on re the Royal Family, and in particular the new uncrowned King Edward VIII and his lady friend Mrs. Wallis Simpson. Well, on the Thursday evening the climax came. In a broadcast Edward made it clear that he would give up the throne and be exiled from his country rather than give up Mrs. Simpson. Personally, I was pleased he made that decision. I always thought what a popular and nice man he was, but too easy-going and not strong enough a character to make a good king. I thought Stanley Baldwin, the Prime Minister at the time, showed great strength of character throughout the crisis. Early in the morning, December 12th, the ex-king sailed out from Portsmouth en route for Boulogne in France on the destroyer Fury, and a few hours later his brother, the Duke of York, took the accession oath and became King George VI.

The following June 3rd, Edward, who was now Duke of Windsor, married Mrs. Wallis Simpson in a chateau near Monte, a small town in France.

One Saturday afternoon in the early 1950s, the Duke and Duchess of Windsor were seen in Campden going into Mr. Rex Morris's newsagent and book shop next to Dover's House. The news soon got around, and my wife Millie, with Mrs. Tom Hooke, walked by them several times as they came along the street. I missed all this, as I was watching a football match in the Recreation Ground.

In May 1937, when King George VI and Queen Elizabeth were crowned, Campden put on another celebration day. As usual on these occasions Campden always has a very full and varied programme, including ox roast, sports, etc., and a large parade through the streets. Once again I drove Pyments' lorry in the parade, and had first prize for the best dressed vehicle. Again I was a member of the winning tug of war team, but the prize this time was a small barrel of beer. I wasn't interested in that.

In November 1937 Edwin ("Ted") Ladbrook died aged 74. He was one of the best known men in Campden and the surrounding district. He was a pork butcher by trade, and always considered a good judge of cattle and pigs, and could estimate the weight of a carcase with great accuracy. My father always had him to kill and cut up our pigs. The pigs were always killed on a bench, and old Ted always brought his terrier dog with him named "Cocky" - he always sat under the bench and drank the blood as it came out. There was always several of us lads stood around when he took the intestines, etc., out, waiting to have the pig's bladder. When he took it out it was full of urine, and he would suddenly swing it around, swilling the urine over us. The bladder we would blow up like a balloon, and tie it on a stick (Norman Morrey uses one with the Campden Morris Dancers). "Ted" Ladbrook was a very witty man, and exceptionally good natured. If there was a bad spell of weather in the winter, he would run his own soup kitchen where anyone was welcome to a drink of good hot soup. He had been married twice, and left a widow and two sons, Charlie and Lawrence. He was fond of all sports, particularly hunting, and always for many years was a "puppy walker" for the North Cotswold Hunt.

About a fortnight after the death of Mr. Ladbrook another notorious old Campden character died, Polly Waine. I don't think they ever established her correct age, but her daughter, Mrs. Taplin, said she was ninety eight. I can remember when I was about nine or ten years old seeing her run in the women's race at Scuttlebrook, so she must have been around eighty years old then. I have heard my father and other old men say her husband John Waine was a large, powerful man, who was scared of nothing, only Polly - she could manage him alright. Mrs. Waine's father, William Baylis, was a Campden man who fought at the Battle of Waterloo. He was born in 1792, and as a young man enlisted at Worcester in the 39th Regiment of Foot. After the Battle of Waterloo he was sent to India until November 1836. Altogether he served nearly twenty four years in the Army. He was discharged as unfit when he was forty-six years old. His army pension was one shilling and two pence halfpenny per week. Mrs. Waine lived in the Almshouses the last few years of her life, but not long before she died she fell and broke her thigh, and went to live with her daughter in Aston Road, where she died. Her granddaughter, Nora Taplin, still lives on her own, in the same house. She is well over eighty, and very active. I see her most days with her little dog, when I am going or coming back from my allotment* .

All my life I have always had a bet, particularly in important races, and the Epsom Derby has always been a lucky race for me (I backed all Steve Donaghue's winners), and I can well remember backing Mid-day-

---

* *She has since died, in 1988.*

73

Sun when it won the Derby in 1937, because it was owned by Mrs. G.B. Miller, the first lady owner ever to own the Derby winner.

The first real race meeting I went to was with my Uncle Bob. I was fifteen at the time, and he took me to Stratford-on-Avon Races. I remember we met "Peggy" Stevens on the course. Peggy was a travelling showman who always had his coconut shy, etc., at Scuttlebrook Wake. He told us that Tom Rimell, who had recently moved his horses from Newmarket to Kinnersley near Worcester, was running a horse that day in the "Selling" race, because he wanted to get rid of it and was expecting it to win. I know I gave Uncle Bob five shillings to put on it (that was all I had), and Uncle Bob put £2 on. The "Selling" race is always the first on the card, and Tom Rimell's horse came first at seven to one. I felt like a millionaire when Uncle Bob gave me my winnings. I was too scared to have another bet, in case I lost some of it.

I never went racing again until 1939 when I decided I would like to go to Cheltenham Races on Gold Cup Day. Me and Fred Rogers cycled to Honeybourne Station where there was a special train going to the Racecourse Station; it was only two shillings and nine pence return fare. I had bad luck on the first two races. The third race was the Gold Cup, and I was stood by the bookmakers trying to make my mind up what to back when a man rushed up and had fifty pounds to win on "Brendan's Cottage", so I didn't hesitate, I put ten shillings on - my normal bet would have been half-a-crown. It was a very exciting race; at the final jump there were three horses almost together, but Brendan's Cottage gradually forged ahead and won at the good price of nine to one. Again I resisted the temptation to back again, and kept my winnings intact.

Towards the end of May in 1938 a Wolseley car driven by Miss Phyllis Neilson-Terry mounted the pavement and crashed into Ellis's shop window. She was accompanied by her famous actress mother, Julia Neilson-Terry. Neither of the famous actresses was seriously hurt. Miss Phyllis Neilson-Terry was appearing in the production of Macbeth at Stratford-on-Avon.

In December 1938 two well-known old Campdonians died. Benjamin Benfield died aged 65 years. For nearly thirty years he drove the horsedrawn bus to and from Campden Station for the landlord of the Noel Arms, Albert Tanner. When Mr. Tanner left Campden, Ben carried on for the new landlord, Mr. Berry. When Mr. Berry took over the British Camp Hotel at Malvern, old Ben went with him, but eventually came back to Westington where he lived. About two days after Ben

74

Benfield died, Harry Ellis passed away aged eighty two years. Mr. Ellis had been married twice. His first wife died in 1895, leaving him with seven children. He married again, and had another family of six by his second wife. Mr. Ellis was born at the "Barley Mow", where his father was in business as a basket maker. He carried on the business of basket making, and employed several of the Hathaway family in his workshop. The main part of the business was making pot hampers and half pot hampers for the market gardening industry. These hampers were oblong, about twenty inches high, and were used for transporting all types of vegetables and fruits before bags were introduced. The second Mrs. Ellis carried on her own fishmonger's and crockery ware shop, quite apart from Harry Ellis's business. H.G. Ellis was always associated with Scuttlebrook Wake, and was a founder member of the old Reading Room, which had its headquarters in the lower room of the Town Hall. He was a staunch patriot and royalist.

During 1938, when Adolph Hitler and his gang of thugs were bullying and gradually taking over territories on their borders, and poor Neville Chamberlain was doing all he could to stabilise the situation, there was a great wave of patriotism throughout the country. In the North Cotswolds a decision was made to form a Territorial Regiment* . In Campden, the headmaster of the Grammar School, Captain Bright, and Major Will Hart were delegated to take charge of and start a unit. Notices were put out, and a room was provided in Scudamore Griffiths' house (Bedfont House). Anyone interested could go and "sign on". I went up straight away, but Mr. Bright said I was the third - George and Henry Hart were the first two. I don't know the official figures, but I can remember twenty seven names, which I thought was very good from a place the size of Campden. The headquarters were at Moreton-in-Marsh, which was about central for the area. During the light evenings the drills were once a week, and at first I used to cycle there. Later Mr. Oliver Beadle, who lived at Berrington Mill, used to take me in his car. We had no uniforms, just an arm band and a Glengarry side hat.

Towards the end of 1938 Mother's health began to deteriorate and, like a good many elderly people, she wouldn't see a doctor, but eventually I persuaded her to have Dr. Birch to come and look at her arm, which was troubling her. She insisted it was rheumatism, but agreed to the doctor coming and seeing her. He came one evening after

* *This was one of the new anti-aircraft gunner regiments, hurriedly formed that year to help counter the menace posed by Hitler's Luftwaffe.*

tea so that I could be there. When he left, he called me outside and said would I agree to let Dr. Leslie from Evesham come to look at Mother; it would cost five pounds. Of course I agreed, and he brought Dr. Leslie a couple of days later. I was not allowed in the room, but when Dr. Leslie had finished examining and questioning Mother, he told me they would be fetching Mother into Evesham Hospital the following morning, as Mother's arm was badly infected with a cancer and she would have to have her arm taken off. She was taken to Evesham the following morning as arranged, and the day after that the ambulance brought her home again with her arm in plaster. Doctor Birch came to see me and told me they did not take her arm off because her stomach was full of cancer. Poor mother lingered on until February 10th, 1939; she had wasted away to just skin and bone. It was pitiful to see her.

Between my marriage in 1935 and Mother's death, each summer I used to hire a car from Luther L. Faringdon's garage in Evesham on a Sunday, and take Mother and my family to Weston-Super-Mare for the day. Occasionally Millie's mother, Mrs. Clifton, would come with us. On one occasion I took them to Whipsnade Zoo, and then carried on to Hemel Hempstead to visit my brother and his wife. Just after leaving Whipsnade Zoo I ran out of petrol. I managed to get to a phone, rang up Bill, and his father-in-law, Mr. Tom Mortimer, came straight away with a two gallon tin of petrol. Garages were few and far between in those days. I used to cycle to Evesham early on a Sunday morning, pick up the car, and then cycle back home in the evening after taking the car back. The hire of the car was £1 per day if you returned it before nine o'clock in the evening.

During the month of May 1939 three of Campden's oldest men died.

George Grove, aged 83 years, member of an old family of stonemasons. "Derby" Grove had worked on the Earl of Gainsborough Estate all his life, until the Estate was sold up, and after that he worked for several years for F. L. Griggs on Dover's Court.

Thomas Hayden, shoeing and general blacksmith, died about the same time as Mr. Grove. He succeeded his late father, Henry Greening Hayden in the blacksmith's business. He was born in the house in which he died. His death meant there was only one blacksmith left in the parish - that was Tom Barnes[*] , who carried on "Bob" Guthrie's business after his uncle, Robert Guthrie, died. At one time, about forty

---

[*] *Immortalised by H.J. Massingham in "Wold Without End" published by Cobden-Sanderson in 1932. See, for example, pages 22-24.*

76

or fifty years before, there were five blacksmiths' premises in Campden, all flourishing.

Also during May, Campden's oldest male inhabitant died, Thomas ("Long Tommy") Bennett. A very tall man, who for years was one of a gang of local men who went to London each year for several weeks mowing and haymaking, then harvesting, before the days of reaping machines. He was also a skilled timber faller. One of the old type, who could do any job in the country.

3. The War

On August 24th, when the situation in Europe was worsening day by day, our Territorial unit was called out to stand by to be ready for active service. The following day we all had to report to the post office, and were given five pounds each, and the next few days we were drilling and having lectures. On August the 31st, at very short notice, we had to say good-bye to our families and were transported in buses to Patchway, on the outskirts of Bristol. The Regimental headquarters were established at a large mansion near Thornbury, and our battery headquarters were in a large house near Filton Aerodrome, and our tents were in the fields along the side of the railway line. Our object was to mount a day and night guard on the flat roofs of the Bristol Aeroplane Factory at Filton, in case the Germans decided to bomb it. If they had we would have been helpless, the only armament we had was two Lewis guns. They only fired .303 bullets, the same as a rifle.

I well remember September 3rd, the day war was declared. Everyone gathered in the works canteen, and when the news was given at eleven o'clock we all cheered. We never dreamt we would be away from home for over six years.

The tent I was in was right beside a coal yard, and I got very friendly with Mr. Shergold, the man who owned the coal business. He knew the Cotswolds around Campden quite well; he said if we could get permission any Sunday he would lend me his car, so that two or three of us could spend a few hours at home. Fortunately, on two occasions myself, George Keitley and Bill Smith did manage it.

A few weeks after we had arrived, we had to go to a large depot at Corsham, near Bath, to get our battle dress and equipment. They kept trying different ones on me, but failed to find one that would fit, so I came away with a dress tunic with brass buttons and brass "collar dogs".

Every time we paraded, being tall, with my polished brasses, I stood out. The Sergeant Major, an old Grenadier Guardsman, said I looked like a colonel on parade, and ever after that I was always known as the "Colonel".

One day Captain Napier sent for me and said each battery had been allocated a new three ton lorry, and the following day I was to go to Chilwell, near Nottingham, to collect it - so I became A Section, 301st Battery, 98th Regiment Royal Artillery lorry driver.

Soon after this we moved to Plymouth and took over a gun site with four mobile 3.7 inch anti-aircraft guns. The site was on the top of Rame Head with a lovely view looking over the town of Plymouth. After being there about a week Captain Napier sent for me again and said I had to go and report to the 916 R.A.S. Co. at Fort Wallington, Portsmouth. When I arrived there five other Royal Artillery drivers reported at the same time. Our job was to deliver guns to R.A. units all over the south of England and the Isle of Wight. Our vehicles were old six-wheeled Scammels - they had no windscreens, just a canvas sheet for when it was raining.

One of the other R.A. drivers who slept in the next bed to me came from Southsea, where his father kept a garage. He had his motor-bike with him. One weekend I had a 48 hour pass, and he lent me his motor-bike to come home to Campden. My pass started at six o'clock in the evening. It was dark when I got to Andover, but I was getting on well until I got to East Ilsley, a village on the Berkshire Downs between Newbury and Wantage. There the old bike "conked out" nearly outside the village pub; I arranged with the landlord to put the motor-bike in a stable at the back of the pub. By this time the landlord had seen the village constable, who said "Come with me, and we will stop a car at the crossroads". Eventually a car came. The constable explained what had happened. It was a man and his wife on their way home to Oxford. They were very kind, took me home with them, gave me a jolly good supper, and the husband said he would take me to Oxford Station early in the morning in time to catch the mail train to Campden. I was home at a quarter to ten the next morning. I had to return to Portsmouth by train, of course. A few days later one of the R.A.S.C. drivers had to take some stores to Newbury, so he went on to East Ilsley and collected the motor-bike.

When the gun distributing was completed we had to return to our units. I returned to the 301st battery, who were now stationed at Saltash, the opposite side of Plymouth to Rame Head. Soon after, the regiment went to Manobier in south Wales for a fortnight's gunnery and firing

78

course. After the course we moved into Raglan Barracks in Devonport, part of Plymouth. Whilst we were there, during an air-raid, two bombs dropped on the barracks, but fortunately not on the wing we were in.

We were then equipped with our own 3.7 inch guns, predictors, range finders, and everything to make us fully mobile. The gun towing vehicles we were issued with were American S.U.'s, petrol driven, and only doing eight or nine miles to the gallon. After about three months they were withdrawn; it was discovered there was a weakness in the rear axles. They were replaced with A.E.C. Matadors, diesel wagons.

From now on we were frequently being moved around, staying only a few weeks in most places. From Raglan Barracks we went to Bude in Cornwall; then to Addlestone in Surrey, where my brother and his wife came to see me one Sunday. From there we moved to Margate on the South Coast; Worksop near Sheffield; Tonfaneau, north Wales; Pen-y-bont, mid-Wales; Manchester area, where we occupied gun sites in Heaton Park, Sale, Altrincham, Stockport, Eccles, and Wilmslow. From there we moved south again to Salisbury, then Leigh-on-Sea, Canvey Island, up the East Coast to Cromer, Grimsby, New Holland, Colchester, and Nottingham. We went to Sheerness on the South Coast for target practice, the targets being towed by very fast speed boats. We had very narrow escapes during air-raids, particularly at Margate, where we were dive-bombed by Stuka bombers, and Weybridge in Surrey, where Messerschmidts dived at us right out of the sun.

We had just settled in at Grimsby when the order came to pack up immediately and go to Alyth in Perthshire, Scotland. There we were attached to the Guards Armoured Division, with orders to be prepared to embark for Spain at a moment's notice. We found out afterwards that Hitler was contemplating taking Gibraltar and continuing down through Spain. Anyway, it did not materialise, and after three weeks of extensive manoeuvres, mostly at night, we were on the move again, this time to Salisbury, because it was thought the German Air Force would try and destroy the cathedral.

In 1941 whilst we were at Addlestone I had been made a lance-bombardier. Then at Heaton Park, Manchester, I got my second stripe to bombardier. Now, at Salisbury, I had a row with Lieutenant Price for refusing to let my limber gunner polish the brasses on the gun, because I said the sun shining on the polished brasses would be easily noticed by aircraft. Lieutenant Price said I would be reported for disobeying orders. The following morning the soldier on telephone duty came to the gun pit to say Major Morby wanted to speak to me. I went to the phone. Major Morby said, "Is that Sergeant Coldicott speaking?" I said, "No, sir, Bombardier Coldicott." He said, "As from now you are Sergeant, it will be on Regimental Orders straight away."

From Salisbury we camped in some woods about two miles out of Colchester, where we had three weeks of very intense commando training. It was very tough, and quite a few who were not quite up to it were posted to a holding unit, and then sent to mixed units (soldiers and ATS).

I had a bit of trouble in Colchester one night with a military police sergeant. It was a nasty wet night, and I had my greatcoat collar turned up. This M.P. stopped me, and told me to put my collar down, which I did, but put it up again when he was gone. Sometime later, going around a corner I met him again. He started to tell me off. I didn't like his pompous manner, and said to him "Why the hell did they put collars on for, if they weren't to be used." He said he was putting me under arrest for insolence and defying his order. He went to take his whistle out, but before he could blow it I belted him one right in the solar plexus as hard as I could. Down he went, gasping for breath, and I very soon disappeared as quick as I could. I have often thought I would love to meet him again, and tell him what I thought of him. He was a right b-----d.

When we were at Weybridge in Surrey I was driving a lorry to a depot near Leatherhead to collect a load of jerry cans of petrol. It was a lovely clear summer's day. I pulled on to the grass verge to watch an air battle between some Messerschmidts and some of our Spitfires. As one of the enemy planes came spiralling down the pilot baled out and drifted down, eventually landing in the field about fifty or sixty yards from me. I dashed to the gate and ran to him; he wasn't injured, but seemed very frightened. He looked to be quite young, probably about eighteen. Coming across the field about two hundred yards away were a party of soldiers. They turned out to be Royal Corps of Signals, who were camped nearby, so of course they took the poor fellow across to their camp. I still have a piece of silk rope from his parachute.

One Sunday morning, whilst we were still at Weybridge, the guard commander sent a message to say there was someone to see me. It was my brother Bill and his wife. They had motored over from Hemel Hempstead. I went to see Major Edwards, told him, and he signed a pass for me to go out for the rest of the day. When we were returning in the evening, as we were approaching Slough, the air-raid sirens started up, so I said to Bill and Edna, "You get off back home, I can get a bus from Slough to Weybridge." They had not been gone long before the bombs started dropping. I had just found a bus stop and had joined the queue, when all at once we heard this bomb coming down at us. We all lay flat on the pavement, and the bomb dropped in the yard of the public house the opposite side of the street from us. Fortunately, none of us waiting for the bus were hurt much, only cuts from broken glass. The blast had blown out all the windows around us, and half the pub was completely demolished. I started to walk to Weybridge, but luckily two military police in a jeep stopped and dropped me off about a quarter of a mile from our camp. About a fortnight later Bill went to Watford and volunteered for active service. He was now in the R.A.F , and 38 years old.

Before I go any further, I must say about my first seven-day leave. It was whilst we were on Rame Head, near Plymouth. No one had been on leave, so to be fair the battery commander Major Freer ordered that all names should be put into a box and drawn out. Well, for once I was unlucky, my name was one of the last out. When the list was put up on orders, Ronnie Trollope, a Somerset lad who had been a groom at Campden House for Mr. Naumann, came to see me, and said he was in the first batch to go on leave, but he would be quite pleased to change with me, as he was single and I was married. I argued with him, but he was quite adamant, so we made an appointment to see Major Freer, who was quite willing to make any alterations providing both parties were agreed. So I came home, and had a good seven days. I am very sad to say poor Ronnie never had a leave. He was posted to another unit, taken ill, and died in hospital. I am not saying it because he was good to me, but he was one of the nicest lads I have ever known.

The first course I went on was a Drill Instructors' course at Fleetwood in Lancashire. I was billeted on the Pier, and occupying the next bed to me was Billy Tansy, the British and European featherweight boxing champion. Whilst there I found lodgings for Millie (my wife), and Betty, who was then about seven years old. They came and stayed a week. I could only see them in the evenings, and they spent most of the days in Blackpool, which was only twenty minutes on the tram. It was a tough course, but I passed out as a Qualified Drill Instructor. Then I went on a week's motor-cycle course, riding out nearly every day over the mountains and valleys in North Wales. We would be out riding for hours without seeing a decent road. At the end of the course the calfs of our legs were blue with bruises, because of so much riding stood up.

My next course was a gunnery course at Stoke-on-Trent. It was a ten day course, and very interesting. When we came away we knew every little nut and spring on the 3.7 inch, all about velocity, wind speeds, etc. and how to change the barrel. On returning to the battery I had to lecture the gun teams - and officers, for some of them didn't hardly

81

know the breech from the barrel. This course finished on the Friday. I had to get back to Salisbury by train. When the train stopped at Worcester Station, I suddenly thought "Why not go home for the week-end", so I rushed out, caught a train to Campden, had a lovely two and a half days at home, and returned to Salisbury on the Monday, no questions asked. The only other course I went on, in England, was a driving course on G.T.V.'s (Gun Towing Vehicles). We were all billeted in a large hotel on the sea front at Rhyl, in north Wales. It was a ten day course which I found quite easy, as I had plenty of experience towing guns. As soon as I was settled in I sent a message home for Millie and Betty to come at once for a week. I found them some "digs" in a house close to where I was billeted. I remember one evening we went to the cinema and saw James Cagney in "Yankee Doodle Dandy", a very good film.

It was whilst we were near Salisbury that we saw our first American soldiers. My limber gunner, a red-headed Scotchman named Bert Laing, was soon in trouble. He and two or three more from our unit went into a pub one night where there were several Americans. Apparently, one asked him what colour our flag was. Bert said, quite innocently, "Red, white and blue". The G.I. said, "I thought there was a yellow streak in it." At that, Bert hit him, nearly knocking him over the bar. Bert was court martialled and went to glass house at Aldershot for twenty-eight days. "Glass house" was the common name for Army prison. Personally, all the G.I.'s I had anything to do with were very decent fellows. What may have caused some friction was the fact that they drew much more pay than our lads.

My wife's pay for herself and Betty was twenty-six shillings a week, and fourteen for myself, so straightaway I signed a form so that she had half of my pay. That left me with seven shillings a week. When I got my first "stripe" I had a rise in pay; again when I was made bombardier; and quite a decent rise when I was made sergeant. But I still allowed Millie half; that was the maximum you could allow.

When the flying bomb, or "Doodlebugs" as we called them, started to fall on and around London, we were sent to a site near Rye in Sussex, but the trouble was, our radar couldn't track them because they were flying too low to be picked up on the screen. Several times I have seen our fighter planes fly alongside of them, and just touch them with their wing tip, which upset the automatic pilot in them and caused them to come down in open country.

When we were issued with 21st Army Group shoulder flashes, we knew we were then under the command of General Montgomery, and

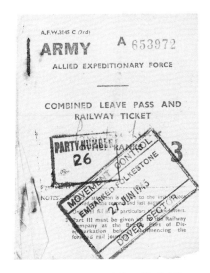

Fred "Colonel" Coldicott.
"Portsmouth, 1939."

Brother, Bill Coldicott, in R.A.F. uniform.

were destined to go into Europe when any invasion took place.

Our next move was back up to Scotland, this time to Rothesay, on the island of Bute off the west coast of Scotland. Here we had to practice loading and unloading all our guns, lorries, etc., and also how to waterproof all the vehicle engines. The boats were specially-built invasion craft, designed so that the guns and all vehicles could be driven on and off in the minimum of time.

When this course was completed, we made our way down through England to Lewes on the south coast of Sussex. On the way, one tea time, we pulled into a farm in the village of Warmington, about sixteen miles from Campden between Tysoe and Banbury. I found out we were staying there for twenty-four hours, saw the orderly officer, and explained to him how close we were to home. He said, if we could find our own transport, he didn't mind where we went so long as we were back in camp by 23.59 hours. My army mate then was Lance Sergeant "Shammy" Folkes, whose home was in Broadway. In the morning we went to the Vicarage to ask the Vicar if he knew where we could borrow a couple of bicycles. He took us to a house, and the lady there said her husband, who was in hospital in Banbury, had a motorcycle and side-car, but she thought the tax had run out. I said that didn't matter, being soldiers we were exempt from tax (we weren't, of course). So we set off. I took Shammy to Broadway, arranged to pick him up about eight o'clock in the evening, and had a good day at home. I knew there wasn't enough petrol to take us back, so I found "Pip" Benfield, who was then driving Pyments' lorry. He said there was about a gallon in a can used for the concrete mixer; he got that for me, so we were okay. I picked my mate up, as arranged; we got back safe and sound, so the little expedition was a complete surprise and success.

When we arrived at Lewes we took over the race course, including the stands and other buildings. The race course is up on the Downs, looking down into the town. After a few days, orders were received that all 21st Army personnel were to be confined in their camp and forbidden to travel anywhere. We all realised then, of course, that time was getting short. Everything that could be loaded was put in the lorries ready for a quick move. On the actual "D" day, all sergeants and officers had what was called "O" groups, where we were informed what was taking place. Then our orders came to pack up and be on the move as soon as possible. When our convoy had gone a few miles we were halted, and a dispatch rider came down the column saying all officers and sergeants were to go immediately to the front of the convoy. When we were all assembled the Colonel informed us that we were on our

84

way to Gosport, where we would load up on "Invasion Barges" and sail for "Juno" beaches at Arromanches on the Normandy coast. We arrived at Gosport, loaded up, and set sail at about eleven thirty at night. Each barge had an anti-aircraft balloon attached to it, in case we were dive-bombed. When dawn came in the morning the barge I was on had lost its barrage balloon during the night. It took us ten hours before we arrived at Arromanches. We had to make a wide detour into the Atlantic because of German "E" boats in the Channel. When we sailed from Gosport, we were issued with blue paper bags to be sick into. I know I used all mine. I had been sick all night, and when we waded ashore I felt awful. As soon as we got everything safely on the beach and assembled, the cooks got organised; we had a good meal, a couple of cups of "char" tea, and everyone was soon back to normal.

As we progressed through Normandy, our feelings were that the locals were not particularly pleased with us. Several times, where Allied and German soldiers were buried, the local people put flowers on the German graves. At one little village, I remember it was called "Thurly-sur-Orne", there were two snipers in the steeple of the village church. They were causing havoc by shooting officers. Evidently, the locals were keeping them supplied with food and water. Our battery was ordered to destroy them, so we had no option but to blow them out, which we of course did. When we crossed over into Belgium, everything changed. We were really made welcome. When we drove into Ostend the people simply mobbed us; we had to come to a halt. They were jumping into the vehicles, and really going "mad". The Dutch people in Holland were just as pleased to see us, but not so excitable as the Belgians. My personal thoughts were, that they were very clean and hard-working people.

In the Spring of 1945 we took part in the defence of Antwerp from flying bombs, or as we called them, "Doodlebugs". Antwerp was then, of course, the most important port in Europe. They came quite frequently for several weeks. When we were in England our success rate at destroying them was about thirty per cent, but in the Antwerp attacks the percentage was nearly ninety per cent. General Montgomery sent a letter of congratulations to General Anderson, in charge of the Anti-Aircraft Defences.

One Saturday evening myself and Charlie Godden, another sergeant, had a lucky escape. We had a few hours off and went into the town in a Liberty Wagon. There was a large theatre in the centre which had been taken over by the Forces as a garrison theatre; there was a Variety on, and we decided to go. When we got there the show had started. It was a packed house; we could only get just inside the door. It was alright for me, but Charlie, who wasn't very tall, couldn't see a thing, so we decided to leave and find a café and get some supper. We walked down towards the docks, and went into a café, and almost the first person I saw was Bert ("Noggin") Keyte, a Campden lad who I went to school with (the same lad who bolted back down Aston Hill the night we were cycling home from Evesham). We had been in the café quite a while talking to Bert, when suddenly there was one hell of a bang, the whole place shook, and the lights went out. When we walked back to the centre it was just chaos. The garrison theatre had a direct hit from a flying bomb. They had two search lights playing on the scene, ambulances were coming and going, and the Pioneer Corps were just arriving with bull-dozers. We heard afterwards that the death toll ran into hundreds. I often thought it was a lucky thing that Charlie Godden wasn't as tall as me. I found out later, when reminiscing with my brother Bill, that he was in Antwerp that night.

Before the war, when living at Midland Bank House, a Mrs. Bennett-Clarke lived opposite, and she had a companion-housekeeper named Marie Vinn. Marie was friendly with us, and often came in for a cup of tea. When we were near Antwerp, I had a letter from home in which was the name and address of Marie Vinn's brother, who was living in Antwerp, so one day me and my mate Shammy Folkes went and found the house, knocked at the door, and as soon as the door opened I knew it was the right place, as inside the hall was a painting of Campden Market Hall. Mr. Vinn and his wife were so excited when I showed him the letter I had received. I never saw poor Marie again, she died with cancer before the war was over.

I have over-run my story, really, so I must go back to when we were at a village in Belgium named Zetrud-Lumay. Our headquarters were established in a large house about half a mile from our gun-site. I left my bombardier in charge of the gun team so that I could go back to headquarters and have a bath. As I was going up the drive to the house, Charlie Rose, our dispatch rider, was coming out on his motor-cycle. He pulled up to ask how I was getting on. He said he was on his way to deliver a dispatch to Regimental Headquarters in Brussels. My wife Millie's cousin Margo Marcelle and her family were living in Brussels. I had the address with me, in case I ever got the opportunity to be in Brussels. I explained this to Charlie, and suggested he took me on the pillion. He eventually agreed, and off we went. He knew where the Headquarters were, he had been twice before, so when he had delivered the dispatch we had to find out where 85 Rue J. Benaets, Uccle 3 -

Margo's address - was. I made inquiries at the tram depot outside the Gare du Nord, where they explained it would be best for us to follow a number 23 tram which went to the district called Uccle. Well, we found it without too much difficulty. When I knocked at the door, a girl about twelve years old came, it was Margo's daughter. Fortunately, they could all speak some English; Margo herself had worked in London for quite a while before she was married. I can't tell you how thrilled they were at seeing their "English Cousin". Charlie Rose and myself stayed with them for nearly an hour. There was Margo's father, Margo, Freddie (her fourteen year old son), and Christiane, her daughter; her husband had died. We arrived back at Zetrud-Lumay OK, but I never had my bath after all. Charlie told the Quarter Master Sergeant he had had a puncture.

After having had a long hard time helping to clear the German Forces off the Dutch islands of South Beveland, North Beveland and Shouen we were brought back for a rest period to a very small village somewhere near Segraven Polder. It was getting close to Christmas, and we decided to save up any chocolate, etc., that we could, to give the children a little treat. Then one morning the orders came - Pack up immediately - and we were on our way to join the 51st Highland Division en route for the Ardennes where Von Rundstedt had driven straight through the American Sector. This was the last occasion where the Germans used airborne troops, but it wasn't a very powerful force; by this time they were having difficulty with supplies, particularly petrol. After the Ardennes breakthrough had been dealt with satisfactorily, we returned to Holland, and after a few days we received orders to hand in all our anti-aircraft equipment, including the guns. We took it all and left it on a captured German airfield. We were to have a few days' rest before joining the 3rd Canadian Infantry Division. I went and saw Major Thorne, our C.O., told him about our relatives in Brussels, and managed to get a seventy-two hour pass, hitch-hiked to Antwerp where I got a train to Brussels. I spent a lovely two days with Margo and her family, and I also spent a few hours with her sister Marie, whose husband had his own printing business; they had two little girls, one about four years, and one about six. All eight of them came to the Gare du Nord Station to see me off on the return journey.

I got on very well with the Canadian soldiers. I knew my cousin Tom Haines's son was somewhere in Europe with the Canadian Forces, but he must have been in some other Division. After I was demobbed, I found out he had spent a leave in Campden with his grandmother, Aunt Julie.

I shall never forget the first time I crossed the Rhine. We crossed over on a pontoon bridge, and on the opposite side there must have been a very large wooded area, but there wasn't a single tree left, only rows of stumps about two or three feet high. Our artillery had smashed everything.

When the war in Europe ended we were camped on the mainland in North Holland at the end of a narrow causeway. About half a mile along the causeway there were about two or three hundred Germans, who had several field guns. The situation was very delicate: if the causeway was damaged in any way, it would have meant thousands of acres of good fertile land would be flooded, together with several villages.

The Germans were very methodical. Every day they would shell us at ten o'clock in the morning and again at four o'clock in the afternoon. We had dug slit trenches some way from our tents, and we took cover in these whilst the shelling took place. Quite a number of the German shells never exploded. We always thought this was due to sabotage in the German factories. Two days after the cessation of hostilities had been declared, about three o'clock in the afternoon, a white flag appeared, and they all came marching towards us in a very orderly fashion. They looked very frightened as they approached us, and I think they were surprised at the humane way we treated them. There were quite a few Dutch traitors amongst them, and these we stripped of everything, watches, rings, etc. I had three watches which I sold here when I came home on leave.

Now the fighting was over, Major Thorne said, "We have had it rough, so now we will take it easy for a while," so he took me and Sergeant Cowcher with him back to a fairly large village named Witmarsum. Here he commandeered the two schools and village hall for "other ranks", and billets in private houses for officers and sergeants. At one end of the village there was a nice looking house painted white; when me and Harold ("Slug") Cowcher knocked at the door, an elderly lady came. When we spoke, she answered in perfect English, and seemed so pleased to see us. We told her we would be billeting ourselves with her for a short time; she was delighted. She was the widow of the local veterinary surgeon.

Whilst talking to her, she enquired what part of England we came from. When I told her Chipping Campden, much to my surprise she said she knew it well. She had been a student at Oxford, and on three occasions had stayed the night in Campden whilst touring the Cotswolds. Unfortunately, our stay in Witmarsum soon came to an end. After three days we were ordered into Germany to take over a large military camp on the outskirts of Wilhelmshaven, the German naval port.

Soon after our arrival at Wilhelmshaven, our regiment had to supply a fifty strong detachment to take part in a victory parade through the town. Being tall, I was one of the chosen. It was a marvellous parade; must have been over half a mile long. There were four bands - two brass, one American and one British; 51st Highland Division Bagpipes; and a Drum and Fife Canadian Band. All the German population were ordered out of their houses to watch us march past. On the outskirts of the town was a large sports field where we were inspected by the Divisional, Corps and Regimental Commanders. I enjoyed every second of it. To hear a military band always makes my "blood race".

About half-a-mile from the camp we were in was an internment camp full of Russians in civilian clothes. Apparently, they had not been anti-German and had been working in Germany; they had created a problem, as no one wanted them. They were a nuisance to us because they were always fighting amongst themselves, and we had to keep sending men in to restore order. The trouble was, none of them could speak English. They appeared to me to be uneducated peasants. I remember one night we had to go in, and we found a man's head in a bucket.

There were other camps containing these Russians in Germany, and eventually they were returned to Russia, where that communist "murderer" Josef Stalin ordered them all to be shot. Whatever they had done was insignificant compared to the crimes of Stalin himself.

We were leading a very lazy life now the war was over. I found it very boring, and then an order was put on the Regimental noticeboard saying there was a shortage of N.C.O.'s in the Burma Campaign, and asking for volunteers to go there. I immediately put my name down, along with a pal of mine, Sergeant "Dick" Dandie, who was then about twenty three years old. I was turned down because of my age, I was then thirty five, but "Dick" went. (One Sunday morning in 1977 a knock came on our door. It was Dick Dandie, he had come from Epsom in Surrey to see me; when he left the Army he was a Major). Anyway, as I was saying, life was a bit boring, so I volunteered to be in charge of half-a-dozen Germans doing work around the area such as draining, hedge-cutting, cleaning out ditches, or any job that needed doing. My interpreter was an ex-Sergeant out of Rommel's Afrika Corps; he could speak English quite well. You couldn't wish for a better work gang. They were all fairly young single lads, but I never had the slightest bit of trouble from them. Being a non-smoker, I used to share my cigarette ration amongst them.

General Montgomery issued an order that under no circumstances were the troops to fraternise with the German population. Well, whether that was wise or not I don't know. I ignored it. Me and a pal of mine, "Deuce" Chattaway, used to visit an old German couple; he had been captain of a German ship in the Great War, had been a prisoner of war in a camp near Newcastle. They only had one son, who was killed in North Africa. They were both very well educated, and spoke good English. A very, very nice couple.

One afternoon I was walking from the camp to the town when I met two women. It was quite obvious that one was pregnant. The one that wasn't said in perfect English, "May I speak to you?" I said go ahead, then she said her friend was expecting her baby very soon, and was worrying herself because she could not get any soap to bathe her baby when it arrived. I was convinced it was a genuine plea; they didn't ask for food, but were desperately in need of some soap. I arranged to meet them the following day, and took them some soap, margarine, and some tea; they were overwhelmed. Not long after, I met the one who could speak English. Her friend had got a little daughter, and had received news that her husband, who had been captured by the Russians, was expected home any time.

I had "acquired" a good double-barrel 12-bore shotgun, and a lovely small revolver with a magazine in the handle. As I was now coming home for a ten days' leave, I sold the revolver to a Canadian soldier for three English pound notes, but decided I would bring the shotgun home. On the boat crossing from Ostend to Dover a message was announced over the loudspeakers, saying anyone with any firearms was to hand them in to the Purser's Office; if discovered at the customs you would be sent back to your unit. The stock and the hand-grip were wrapped in some underwear in my valise, and the barrels were well wrapped around in brown paper. When we landed the Customs were stopping one occasionally - I was lucky there, but when we came out of the Customs building we had to walk up an alleyway to the trains. Half way up were two military policemen. I was nearly by them when one grabbed my arm and said, "What have you got there." I said, "The barrel of a gun." He said, "What! Let's have a look." So I tore the paper off the end, and he put his finger in, looked at his mate and said, "It isn't a rifled bore," and his mate said, "OK, let him go." I was damned glad when that train pulled away.

I had a lovely time at home. One day Millie and me hitch-hiked to Birmingham and back; she bought a new coat and had a grand time around the shops. She had been saving up her clothing coupons for when I came home.

On my return journey to Germany, I saw Charlie Rose from Stow-on-the-Wold on Paddington Station, so we travelled together. At Calais in France we had to go to a "holding camp" until we got transport to Germany. When we arrived at this camp I said to Charlie Rose, "You mind our kit whilst I find the 'ablutions' to have a wash." Having found them, I shouted to Charlie to come over. A few moments later someone slapped me on the back; it was my brother Bill, he had recognised my voice when I shouted to Charlie. He went over to England on the same boat as I did, and had just returned on the same boat again - the regulations were, R.A.F. personnel and the troops were to be kept apart. We were not allowed to board the ship until all R.A.F. were on board. They were on one deck, and we on another. Bill was on his way back to Germany also, but his unit was about fifty miles away from Wilhelmshaven. After I had been back a few days I went and saw the woman and her baby girl. Her husband was back home. They were overjoyed to see me, but unfortunately they hardly knew any English.

Before I proceed any further, I must go back to when we were in Holland. It was one of the hardest winters, weather-wise, that we had had for some years. For weeks we had to sleep fully dressed, it was so cold, and the guns had to be traversed and elevated frequently whenever they were not in use, because the frost was so intense that the lubricating oil froze. Back home the Liverpool Docks refused to load the ammunition on to the ships, and came out on strike demanding danger money. At the same time thousands of coal miners, mostly in the Kent coal mines, also came out on strike. All us artillerymen were furious, it makes me red even now when I think about it. It makes me mad when I read in the papers, and see on the television, about the hardships in the Liverpool area. None of the politicians have the "guts" to get up and say that it was Jack Jones and his fellow Union leaders that reduced Liverpool from being the busiest port in Europe to what it is now. Their continual striking diverted all the shipping trade to Antwerp and other ports in Europe.

I was in the Company Office doing the Sergeant-Major's job whilst he was on leave. One morning an order came through from Divisional headquarters asking for the names of anyone interested in going on a refresher trade course being held at Nienberg, near Hamburg. The idea was to give anyone with a trade a refresher before being demobbed. I thought it was a good idea, so I put my name down for a bricklaying and mason's course. About three weeks later I went to Nienberg for a

91

fortnight's course. I should think there was nearly a hundred on the same course as me. The first thing we had to do was draw a plan to scale of a fireplace. All these were collected and examined. Then we were split up into groups of three, and the one with the best plan was in charge. I was in charge of my group, and what happened then was, we were issued with tools and taken on to a large concrete area where we had to construct the chosen fireplaces. After that, when we were not having lectures we were building a recreation room and sergeant's mess. I really enjoyed my time there. It was much better being occupied than leading a lazy existence like we were at Wilhelmshaven.

The Forces were being demobbed in age groups. My group was no. 17, the thirty-five year olds. Our turn came in November. There were sergeants from our unit, and we had always been great pals together: Myself, "Colonel"; Shammy Folkes; and "Trigger" Smith. I shall never forget: we were loaded up in the lorry which was taking us to Hamburg, when the Sergeant Major came, and said I was wanted at the Battery Office. Of course, I immediately thought something was wrong. Anyway, when I went in it was Major Price (who, when he was a lieutenant, we had a row over polishing the brasses on the guns at Salisbury). He said, "Sergeant, I couldn't let you go without shaking hands with you. Several times we have had our differences, but I would like us to part good friends." I thought that was really nice of him. Of course we parted good friends, I was never one to bear malice.

When we arrived at Ostend, we were informed the ship we were to sail on could not depart because of dense fog in the Channel, but things improved the following day, and we got away in the evening. We had to stay the night in Folkestone. The next morning Shammy Folkes and myself were told to report to the de-mob at Taunton in Somerset, and Trigger Smith was bound for Chilwell, because his home was Nottingham. At Taunton we again had to stay the night. The next morning we had to hand our uniforms and equipment in. You had the option to retain your greatcoat or receive £1; I took the pound. Then we went to another large building where we chose our de-mob suit and trilby hat. I arrived at Campden about tea-time, so at last my Army career had come to an end. It was an experience I am glad I had, and I must say I was very unsettled for quite a while, but I knew I was a very lucky man to come back to a good, loving wife and a lovely daughter. My one regret was the fact that I had not been able to share in Betty's bringing-up. I couldn't help feeling I was almost a stranger to her.

92

4. And Since...

After de-mob I was on Army pay for the next month, but I was never one to be idle, so I went sprout-picking most days. Campden Parish Council and some other organisations joined forces and invited all ex-members of the Forces to the Town Hall, where we were presented with five pounds each as a token of thanks for giving our services; I thought it was a very nice gesture. A law had been passed whereby no matter what your job had been when you went into the Forces, you could demand to be given the same job again after you were de-mobbed, so when I eventually went round to see Mr. Pyment he said, "How nice to see you again, I know you will have to have your job back as lorry driver, so I'm afraid I shall have to give "Pip" Benfield his notice to leave." When I told him I wasn't interested in the lorry job anymore he was very relieved. I told him I had passed the course at Neinberg in Germany as a fully qualified mason-bricklayer, so the following Monday I started work again; the tradesman's rate of pay was about threepence per hour more than a lorry driver.

I remember the first job I went on was to build a new large barn and fruit store for Ralph Stanley at Whaddon Farm. There were four tradesmen: myself, George Plested, Jack Pitcher, and Wilson Bennett. One day I was working up the Aston Road when Maurice Keeley pulled up in his car to see how I was getting on. His car was a sixteen horsepower M.G. Magna. After a bit of bantering I bought it off him there and then for seventy-five pounds. It was one of the daftest things I could have done; it was a sports car really, it wasn't too bad for room in the two front seats, but Bet in the back was cramped up with her knees almost touching her chin.

Tom Hooke, who kept the shop across the road from us, had a brother, Ted. He and his wife used to come to Campden occasionally, and we were very friendly with them. During the Summer of 1946 they came to Campden for a holiday, gave us the keys of their home in London, so we went off in the M.G. and had a lovely week in their house. It was in a mews, immediately behind the Cumberland Hotel near Marble Arch. On the ground floor was a garage, so we had no worries about parking the car. It was a lovely holiday, we went to two or three theatres and several museums, including the British Museum. We also went to the Tower, where Bet got very friendly with Mr. Buckland, one of the "Beefeaters".

I have just realised I am getting on too fast with my story, on

93

December 1st, 1945, Mr. Harold Pyment and his wife gave a party at the Kings Arms Pantry for all their friends and employees to welcome home their son, Sgt. Desmond Pyment. For nearly three years he had been a prisoner in the hands of the Japanese. For many months there had been no news of him, and being their only child you can imagine how they must have felt. Then after the war was over, out of the blue they received the news that he was in Australia, in a hospital, reduced to a mere skeleton. And now he was back in Campden nearly fully recovered from his ordeal. I had quite a long talk with him, and he told me that at one time they dug up worms and ate them to keep alive. When he was a youth before the war I taught him to drive; he was a lovely lad, and now he is just the same, a grand fellow.

In March 1946 I went to Cheltenham Races on Gold Cup Day, and every year after until 1970. During these years I witnessed some of the finest race horses that have ever looked through a bridle, such as Golden Miller, Prince Regent, and Arkle. The two outstanding steeplechase jockeys that I have seen were Fred Winter and Johnnie Francombe.

Pyments always seemed to have plenty of work, and I was quite happy. The good thing about the building trade is the variety; you are never too long in one place, and no two jobs are the same.

In 1947 I joined the British Legion. I was never a "drinking" man, but I used to go about two evenings a week to have a game of snooker. It was a good night out in those days, they were a merry crowd. There was Wally Stanley, Jack Mitchell, Joe Haydon, Bernard Righton, Percy Righton, Stale Benfield, Joey James, Bob Grove, etc., all of them dead now. Very often when old Joe Haydon was playing he would take his glass eye out, and pretend to use it as a snooker ball.

I was voted on to the Legion Committee, and we decided to form a concert party. For our first effort we gave an open air concert in the Square, dressed like the Black and White Minstrels. It was a great success. There was myself, George Hart, Ted Bennett, Dennis Hughes, Joey James, Tom Davies, Walter Clarke, George Slim, Ray Danter, and Marjorie Ladbrook our pianist. For the next few years we gave concerts at Bourton-on-the-Water (3 times), Evesham, Snowshill (twice), Blockley (twice), and of course on various occasions in Campden. The last two years our pianist was Mrs. Richards. It was a great pity, and I was very disappointed, when we disbanded.

There are three events that stand out in my memory for 1948. First, I took part in a parade of old soldiers in Hyde Park, London, organised by the Royal British Legion. It was a very hot day, and I should think one

94

of the largest parades ever: we were inspected by the Princess Elizabeth and her husband, Prince Philip, who came round stood up in a jeep. Then they stood on a dais whilst the whole parade marched past. We had to stand in the hot sun for so long that people were fainting all over the place.

On May 18th, 1948, I went to a boxing tournament on Coventry City Football Ground. The main contest was between Dick Turpin of Coventry against Boss Murphy from New Zealand for the British Empire Middleweight Championship. Turpin won by a knockout.

Then, on June 28th, I went to another tournament at the Villa Park, Birmingham. This time Rinty Monaghan the flyweight champion of the world beat Charlie Squires, and Dick Turpin successfully defended his middleweight title against Vince Hawkins.

All through the autumn and winter months for the next three years myself, Mr. Pyment, Don Bragg (butcher), Father McCarron (Catholic priest), Mr. Thomason (chemist), and Joe Chamberlain went to the monthly all-in wrestling tournaments at Cheltenham Town Hall. On the way we always called in to the Rising Sun on Cleeve Hill for a drink. I did enjoy those outings; they were grand people to go out with.

Every year, usually at the end of March or first week in April, the Campden Parish Council holds the annual Parish Public Meeting. At this meeting the accounts of all local charities have to be read out. In 1949 I attended the meeting with my pal Val Hobbs. There was a very old charity where money had been left to provide a new jacket for two working men of the parish; the Clerk stated no one had applied for this charity for a great many years.

After the meeting I said to Val, "How about going up to the Vicarage and put in a claim for a jacket each?" Val said he was game, so, although it was then ten o'clock in the evening, off we went to the Vicarage. The Rev. Brian O'Loughlin answered the door himself. We told him the purpose of our visit, he invited us in, and then said, "Of course you two are only joking." When we persuaded him we were serious, he said, "Well, legally you are quite within your rights," so he wrote a letter to Mr. Knott, who was then chairman of the parish council. He gave us the letter, and said, "Take this to Mr. Knott, and he will have to decide what to do about it."

The next evening we took the letter to "Tommy" Knott. Like the Vicar, he said "Are you really serious or having a joke?" We had decided to see it through, now we had gone so far, so we said we were quite serious. Tommy Knott said the best thing to do was for us to purchase a

95

jacket each and let him have the receipts, and he would then pay us back the money.

The following Saturday I bought a lovely check coat from "The Famous" shop in Cheltenham, and Val bought one in Stratford-on-Avon. Tommy Knott gave us a cheque each on giving him our receipts. We have had many a laugh about it over the years, because it really started off as a joke.

Myself, Millie, and Bet went to London for a long weekend, and stayed at the Union Jack Club near Waterloo Station. I am afraid I have forgotten which year it was, but I can remember we visited the British Museum and the Science Museum in Kensington. A few weeks before our visit to London a film company had spent a few days in Campden, shooting scenes for a film called "The Franchise Affair". The stars were Michael Denison and Dulcie Grey, who were husband and wife in real life. On two occasions Millie had ten pounds for taking part as an extra, and got to know Michael Denison and his wife quite well. Whilst we were in London we met them in the street, they recognised us immediately, and we had quite a long chat with them. They really were a grand couple.

In 1950 myself, Millie, Betty, and Millie's mother and sister all went to Belgium for a fortnight and stayed with Margo (Millie's cousin) at Uccle, a suburb of Brussels. Whilst there, we all went to Oudegarde to visit Madame Delarulle-Stordeux and her family, also the nuns at the local convent. All these had been very kind to me whilst we were in that district during the war. Oudegarde is a village about thirty miles from Brussels. We went there by train, and we found the carriages were very poor compared with England. We had a lovely holiday. Margo took us out every day, and it was a great help to us because she could speak in English equally as well as French or Walloon.

The following year, Margo's son Freddie came to stay with us for a few weeks. We went up to London and met him at Waterloo Station, stayed the night at Sussex Gardens, and travelled down to Campden the following day. He was a tall, fine looking lad of fifteen, and thoroughly enjoyed his stay here, being very popular with our local girls.

1951 being one hundred years since the last Dover's Games were held on Dover's Hill, Campden decided to start them up again. A public meeting was held where it was decided that every club or institution in the town should appoint one member to serve on a committee. I was on the committee, representing the British Legion. After a great deal of hard work the great day came on Thursday, May 17th, 1951. It was fortunately a nice fine day, and a huge success, and I am pleased to say it has since become one of the great sporting occasions of the Midlands. For some years professional all-in wrestling was one of the features, and every year myself and Val Hobbs were official seconds in the corners. All the well-known wrestlers appeared, and I looked forward very much to making their acquaintance each year; the majority of them were extremely nice people.

In 1952 I took Millie to Royal Ascot on the Gold Cup Day. It was a lovely warm day, and a great experience; we both enjoyed every minute of it. At that time Gordon Richards (now Sir Gordon) was the champion jockey, and the day before he had not ridden a winner, so I thought he would be sure to have one or two winners. I backed his horse in every race, but again he had a blank day, so I had no luck; but I enjoyed myself. The next day, of course, he rode three winners.

I was enjoying my work at Pyments. Having a car, most of the jobs I did were out of Campden, because I could provide my own transport and take a labourer with me. Of course, they paid me three pence a mile for petrol, etc. On one occasion I had to take and fix a large gravestone in a cemetery at Aylesbury in Buckinghamshire. Of course I had to take the lorry on that trip. The gravestone was in memory of Paul Woodroffe's eldest son. Paul Woodroffe was the well-known stained glass artist who lived at Westington.

One job I was in charge of was some alterations to a farm house at Coleman's Hill, between Hidcote and Admington. There was a large area of gorse bushes on the farm which was full of rabbits, and the farmer said I could have all I could kill, so every dinner time we would go around the farm, and I would shoot some every day. There were usually three or four of us, so we shared the rabbits out; the men were very pleased.

Each year during the game season I was doing very well for pheasants. Sunday mornings I would go off in the car, and was very disappointed if I didn't come home with a brace. Occasionally I had one or two on my journeys to and from work. On one occasion I had the job to put in a new marble fireplace in Batsford House for the present Lord Dulverton's mother. The day I was finishing the job I took my gun, and near the bottom of Draycott Hill I bagged a cock pheasant. Later on in the day, when I was packing my tools after finishing the job, Lady Dulverton came into the room, said she was very pleased with my work, would I like a pheasant. Of course I said yes, so I had to go with the butler to where the pheasants were hung and choose my own; I chose a nice fat hen bird that had not been shot about. I wonder what

97

she would have thought if she had known I had one of her cock birds in the boot of the car.

The first seaside holiday we went on was to Paignton in Devon about 1951. It was really hot the whole week, but unfortunately poor Millie could not stand the sun. Other years we went to Dawlish, Teignmouth, Exmoor, London and Brighton, and every year we would spend a weekend with Millie's old school pal Cissie and her husband Harry Martin at Denton, a village near Grantham.

About this time Bill Hobbs was in business as a market gardener, and Val, his brother, was lorry driver for him. Once a week I used to accompany Val to London to deliver produce to Covent Garden (the old Covent Garden). The market did not open until midnight, so we used to leave Campden about 9 p.m. We were always back in Campden long before it was time for me to go to work. I well remember our first visit to Covent Garden, we were there before midnight and started to unload the lorry. Before we had taken much off, a man and a police constable came rushing up and told us to put back what we had taken off as quickly as we could; the porters came on duty at midnight, and if they found any produce had been unloaded they would immediately come out on strike.

In 1952 my wife Millie had to go to the Radcliffe in Oxford to have a small polypus taken away from the neck of her womb. Our doctor, Charles Moorhead, told her it was quite a simple operation, and she would only stay in hospital for one night. I took her in one morning expecting to fetch her back home the following day, but to my amazement about 7 o'clock in the evening she walked in home: At the hospital they had put her on the train for home. She didn't look very well, so we went to bed early, but during the night she was passing clots of congealed blood. At half past two in the night I went along and rang Dr. Moorhead's night bell. He came to the door in his pajamas. When I started to explain, he said, "Get back home, I'll be there as soon as you are," and he was. He took one look at the blood in the chamber pot and said he must use a phone immediately. I had the Midland Bank keys, so I took him down into the bank (I was living there at that time). He demanded that he must speak to a doctor at once. When the doctor came on, Dr. Moorhead told him he had never before experienced anything so disgraceful, he wanted an ambulance as soon as possible, and he told the doctor, "Make sure you are there to meet it when it arrives." Thank heaven everything turned out alright. The following year Dr. Moorhead's body was found near his car, close to Horseman Corner; he had shot himself. It was a great shock to everyone, a popular and very capable doctor.

My cousin Tom Haines came over from Vancouver Island for about two months to stay with his mother (Aunt Julie). Each Sunday he came and had his Sunday dinner with us at Midland Bank House. He went to Canada with my father in 1905, had eventually settled down in Manitoba, and had now retired to Vancouver Island, having handed over his large farm to his son. He tried to persuade us to go back with him, saying we could stay with him until we had our own place. He reckoned I could make a fortune in a few years, as at that time builders were in such a great demand and could almost charge what price they liked. Anyway, we didn't go, we decided there are better things in life than money.

It was 1951 when our daughter Betty was made the Scuttlebrook Queen. It was a lovely warm day, and she looked marvellous; we felt very proud of her.

Not long after this I was in charge of a job at Crimscote near Newbold-on-Stour. It was to convert a large farmhouse into two separate houses. One day we had to carry some very large blue flagstones up some steps out of the cellars. On the way home, and all that night I realised something was wrong, so I went to see Dr. Olliff the next morning. It was a bad rupture: the doctor said it may be three months' wait before it could be repaired, but he would do all he could to hurry it up. I bought a truss from the chemist's and carried on working, but even with the truss I sometimes had to lie down and push it back into place. It was a great relief when six weeks later I went to the Radcliffe Infirmary in Oxford for the operation. Thank God it has been alright since.

My next visit to a hospital was quite unexpected. We were doing some work for Lord Ebrington at Ebrington Manor. We were using a large concrete mixer that sometimes was very difficult to start. One morning my labourer was trying to start it, but didn't seem strong enough to turn the engine over, and asked me to do it. I gave it a swing, and the next thing I knew I was laying on my back with the gardener's wife bent over me putting a bandage around my head. Afterwards they told me the engine had backfired, flinging the starting handle off, which hit me in the eye and knocked me out. They took me over to Dr. Olliff's, who looked at it and said Cheltenham Eye Hospital straight away. There they gave me an anaesthetic. When I came round the doctor came to see me, and said, "Old boy, you are very lucky, we have had to put four stitches in the ball of your eye, but another one hundredth part of an inch, and you would have lost the sight of your eye forever." I am pleased to say it never left me with a scar, but the sight of that eye has never been very good ever since.

About 1956 - I am not quite sure of the year - myself, George Hart, Lionel Ellis, and Bill Payne were asked by the B.B.C. to do a short sketch for a television show, to go out on the Christmas Eve on the Central Programme. We did the recording in the Fleece Inn at Bretforton. The B.B.C. provided us with a good three course luncheon and ten pounds each. The sketch and dialogue was based on the Campden Mummers' play.

On August the third, 1957, our daughter Betty was married to Robert Grove. It was a lovely day, and a lovely wedding; everything went perfectly. They spent their honeymoon at Yarmouth, and came back to their own bungalow (where they still live). Robert had built the bungalow almost entirely on his own. Thank God he has been, and still is, a real good husband and good father to my three granddaughters.

For quite a few years I took Millie and Mrs. Clifton, her mother, every Saturday afternoon to Evesham. After going around the shops we always went to one of the cinemas, depending where we thought the best film was. I must say, films then were real good family entertainment, but not having been to a cinema for some years now, I won't comment on the modern ones.

One Sunday in 1965 Millie, Gran, and myself went out for a trip around the villages, and we called in at the Riverside Café in Bidford-on-Avon for tea. Millie didn't seem to be her usual cheerful self, so I said was something worrying her; she then started crying, and said she had a small lump in one of her breasts. The next morning I took her to the surgery. Dr. Olliff examined her, and said he would arrange for her to see a specialist at the Radcliffe in Oxford as soon as possible. I took her up to Oxford. The specialist said it was malignant and they would have to take her breast off. Three days later we again went to Oxford, and she had the operation; at the same time they also removed her ovaries. When Millie came home from hospital I took her and her friend Mrs. Chattaway to Hunstanton, left them there for a week, then went and fetched them back home. Unfortunately, the weather had not been very kind to them. A few weeks later I took Millie for a week's holiday to the Lake District. I had written and booked up for a week at Grange-over-Sands. We hardly had any sleep the first night it was so close to the railway, and trains were going by all night. After breakfast the next morning I told the landlady we couldn't stay, because Millie needed to sleep well. She didn't think much of it, but I loaded the car up, and off we went. We called in at a roadside café for a drink, and I got into a conversation with a farmer. I explained our situation to him, he said come and meet my wife and spend the rest of the week with us. This we did, and it turned out to be the best holiday we ever had.

Millie's health soon improved after she had a course of cobalt radium treatment at Oxford, and she seemed to be quite back to normal again. In April 1968 a bad ulcer developed on one of her legs. We informed Dr. Olliff and he said she was to go to bed, and he would come and examine it. When he came down the stairs he said would I go outside with him. He said, "I'm very sorry to have to tell you, Fred, but Millie has only about another six weeks to live." Well, that was the greatest shock I have ever had, it knocked me for six. Poor girl, she hadn't a clue, so I had to carry on a normal life with her. I took her up to the Radcliffe on three occasions for injections. On the first occasion the specialist came to see me whilst Millie was gone with the nurse; he said it was quite true what Dr. Olliff had told me, it was cancer of the liver. Millie was always a very cheerful and happy person, and remained so right up to the end. The night before she died she was talking about having new curtains. The next morning she got up and sat with me whilst I had my breakfast. I was working in Campden at the time, and about ten o'clock Fred Benfield the butcher came to tell me Millie was dead. Our daughter Betty had found her dead on the floor at the top of the stairs. The doctor was there, and he helped me to lift her onto the bed. That was the 17th of June, so when Dr. Olliff said six weeks, his prediction was nearly correct. Thank God Millie didn't suffer any pain.

I found that when it hits you the worst is when the coffin is lowered into the grave; words cannot express how you feel then. After the funeral was over my brother and his wife took me back to Hemel Hempstead with them. I stayed a week, but on my return it was awful going back into an empty house. Whenever I was working close to home I went down to Betty's for my mid-day meal, and for a while most weekends I stayed with my old army pal "Deuce" Chattaway and his wife at Balsall Common near Coventry; they were very kind to me.

Mr. Harold Pyment's health had not been very good for quite a while, and he had taken on Mr. John McNamara (who was an accountant) as his partner. John had previously been in charge of the office where my daughter Betty worked at "Booth and Bomfords", electrical engineers in Evesham. Well, I carried on for a few months, but the firm was no longer a "happy" firm, and after one or two minor rows I finally lost my temper. I told "Mac" I had had enough, and packed up there and then. When I told my pal Val Hobbs, he told Mac if I was finishing that was it, he would pack in as well. The next day we went to Cheltenham to sign on the dole until we obtained another job, and there they told us Mr. MacNamara had rung up to tell them we had "sacked" ourselves, so we could not have any benefit. On my return home, I wrote a letter to the Earl of Gainsborough at Exton Park, telling him that myself and Mr. Hobbs would be starting out on our own, and would be very pleased to put a quote in for any work that might come along on his Campden estate. I received a reply by return of post saying he was pleased we were going on our own, and would we meet his agent at the Court House. We met the agent of course. He took us all over the Court House, and described to us the various jobs that had to be carried out: it was a considerable amount of work. We took the job on a time-and-material basis. We went to Burlinghams in Evesham, had an interview with the manager, and they allowed us a credit of £300 per month for materials. One day Lord and Lady Gainsborough came to see how we were progressing. We said our biggest problem was, we hadn't anywhere to store anything, such as timber, sand, cement etc., so Lady Gainsborough suggested to Lord Gainsborough, why not let us have the large barn, the old Almonry, and the farm-yard. He said, "A good idea", so we were well set up then. Some time later he gave us the job of stripping the roofs off the barn and Almonry, and re-slating them.

One day, whilst renovating an old cottage at Ilmington, a young man who came to inject the walls for dampness said a friend of his at Alderminster had a lorry for sale at a reasonable price. We went the following day to see him. We found out he was going bankrupt, and didn't want a cheque, so we got the lorry very cheap by giving him cash. It turned out a good buy.

We were never short of work, and never had to advertise. When we were very busy, we had to employ other tradesmen, but always on a self-employment basis so that we cut down on office work. Our work was not confined to the Campden area; we had jobs at Oxford, Evesham, Ilmington, Badsey, Balsall Common, Coventry, Ebrington, Wickhamford, and the last three months before we retired we were working on Lord Gainsborough's estate at Withington near Andoversford.

When my wife was in the Radcliffe at Oxford, Mrs. Adams from Paxford was in there at the same time. Her daughter Nancy, who lived with her, had unfortunately been struck down with polio when she was a little girl, and it had left her with a "damaged" foot and leg. Nancy had no means of getting to Oxford, so I took her up with me every evening in my car, for which she and her mother were very grateful. Millie and Mrs. Adams were both discharged on the same day. In April

102

1970 Mrs. Adams died. I liked her very much, she was a very nice person. Nancy, of course, was left on her own, so I persuaded her to come to Campden and look after me. It was the best thing I could have done, I couldn't possibly be looked after better, and she has a wonderful personality - never moody, and very similar in character to Millie. In July 1971 I made my mind up to marry her. I went up to Stow-on-the-Wold to the Registry Office and arranged to be married there on Saturday the 17th. I never told her until tea-time on the Friday (didn't give her time to refuse). Up until now we have had sixteen years of happiness, never quarrelled, and as far as I'm concerned, never will. I have been very fortunate, no one could have had two better wives than I have.

I retired from work in 1979 when I was sixty nine, and I must say I am enjoying my retirement very much. I keep my allotment, and every year I manage to get amongst the prize winners. It is nice to feel free, and be able to please yourself.

On looking back over my life, I consider I have lived through the most interesting period this country and the world have ever known. My early boyhood was in the days of the oil lamps and horse-drawn vehicles, so I have witnessed all the wonderful inventions leading up to the present days of remote control, nuclear energy, and space exploration. Whether it is a better world for all these things I leave you to judge for yourselves.

I will end by saying, I have been very fortunate, and "thank God for everything". The only thing I regret is that I never had a son, but I have a good daughter, and three lovely granddaughters: Carol, Rachel and Amanda.

5. Afterword: 1994

I was 76 years old when I wrote these memories. Now I am 83. Obviously, events in our lives are continuously taking place, so in my case I will bring the memories up-to-date.

I am now a very proud great grandfather. My oldest granddaughter, Carol, now Mrs. Hope, has two lovely daughters, Francesca ("Frankie") aged 6 years and Alexandra ("Alex") aged 3 years. My second granddaughter Rachel, Mrs. McClusky, has a lovely daughter Louise aged 2 1/2 years, and six month old twins Katie and Ben.

103

My only brother Bill died in 1986 after suffering for four years with Parkinsons Disease. Nearly all my schoolmates have passed on, and there are only four of us left in Campden who joined the Territorials in 1938: Wilfred Smith, Thomas Hayden, Ron Gould and myself.

In February 1990, one of my old school pals, Charlie Blake, passed away. Charlie had a lovely disposition, never miserable, with a permanent smile, and was well-liked by everyone. For years me, and Millie my first wife, always met Charlie at Scuttlebrook Wake, had some fun, and a good laugh. I remember when we were young lads, myself, Charlie, Wilf Plested, and Bert Bruce walked over to Paxford, and that was when he first saw Vera Webb, who a year later became his wife.

Ernest Henry, or "Chinese" Wilson as he was known, was born in Chipping Campden on the 15th of February 1876. He was famous for collecting rare plants from China, Japan, Bonin Island, Korea, and Formosa. It was decided to have a memorial garden in Leysbourne to commemorate his achievements. The garden was opened by Roy Lancaster on May 31st 1984. I was invited to meet Roy at the ceremony. It was a scheme I fully supported. I was very much against the Planning Authority's policy of building on every bit of open space.

In 1987 ITV Central Television made a series of twelve programmes called "Home Town", with Roy Hudd as the interviewer. Chipping Campden was one of the towns chosen. The producer met anyone who was interested in the Saddle Room at the Red Lion. I was amongst those chosen. On 21st July 1987 a bus took us to the studios at Nottingham. My wife Nancy accompanied me, and we had a very enjoyable day. At the end of the programme Roy Hudd read an extract from my Memoirs.

During January and February of 1991 I was in Cheltenham and Moreton-in-Marsh Hospitals with a massive thrombosis of my right leg. I could only walk with a frame for several weeks. Then I had crutches for a while, then after using a "thumb stick" I gradually gained confidence, and now I have discarded my stick. I had the gears and accelerator of my motor car put on the steering wheel; and about six months ago I had it returned to normal* . Last year I took over a Council allottment, which keeps me busy, and gives me great pleasure.

In hospital, doctors proposed to remove Mr. Coldicott's leg (to which he said "No"). Once home, it is clear that he was not expected to walk again, much less drive. Through great personal determination and the support of his wife Nancy, he now does both again.

6. Old Local Words

-Bog-: Another name for outside closet.

-Burden-: Several lengths of firewood tied in a bundle.

-Burrow-: Sheltered side of hedge, wall, tree, etc.

-Byunt-: Am not.

-Cagnags-: To "henpeck", or keep talking.

-Clapered-: When your clothes or shoes were very muddy.

-Clomber-: To climb.

-Daddocky-: Decayed wood.

-Dillen-: The smallest pig in a litter, or family.

-Fammel-: Famished, or hungry.

-Flummoxed-: Puzzled.

-Maukin-: An untidily dressed woman.

-Mingy-: Mean, tight fisted.

-Miskin-: The place where kitchen waste and fire ashes were dumped.

-Mollar holt-: Grip, or clutch.

-Momble-: Walk awkwardly.

-Mombley-: Bewildered, or slightly dizzy.

-Mooching-: Wandering about.

-Muckle-: Manure heap.

-Nash-: Delicate or weak.

-Petty-: The earth closet in the garden.

-Scrimpy-: Small or puny.

-Scud-: A sharp shower of rain.

-Sharry-: About a six feet long stake carried on the other shoulder to balance the shoulder stick.

-Shoulder-stick-: Length of wood carried on the shoulder to saw into logs.

-Snoffely-: A cold in the head and nose.

-Unkid-: Dreary, awful.

-Yawp-: Stare at a person, etc.

-Yorks-: Leather straps, or string, worn just below the knee.

-Yunt-: Isn't.

-Yud-: Head.

1. Jim "Mangler" Blakeman	18. Albert "Noggin" Keyte	35. Charlie James
2. George Sharpe	19. Fred "Pecker" Howell	36. Harry Bradley
3. Sid "Sausage" Bridge	20. George Drinkwater	37. Fred "Sortalike" Howell
4. Jack Harris	21. George "Lucas" Greenall	38. Lewis Wheatcroft
5. Cyril "Squirty" Harris	22. Charlie Blake	39. Dudley Wheatcroft
6. Fred "Brawny" Coldicott	23. Louis Wheatcroft	40. Don Wheatcroft
7. Alf Keen	24. Tom Hayden	41. Derek Morrey
8. Fred Keitley	25. Bill "Wiggy" Booker	42. Alan Drinkwater
9. Charlie "Polly" Hayden	26. Percy "Noddy" Pitcher	43. George Phipps
10. Mr. G.W. Dewey	27. Cyril Pouncett	44. Bill "Fag" Turner
11. Les Keeley	28. Alfred Richardson	45. Alwyn Keeley
12. Jack Bickley	29. Ern Bickley	46. "Carrots" Howell
13. Harry Pope	30. Ernie "Mickey" Smith	47. Teddy Smith
14. Wilfred "Timmy" Plested	31. Albert Richardson	48. L. Potter
15. Wilfred "Nunc" Smith	32. Fred "Nibs" Benfield	49. Walter Smith
16. Raymond "Pussy" Weale	33. Walter Drinkwater	
17. Charlie Smith	34. Claude Whalley	

INDEX
of
Memories of An Old Campdonian

Prepared by Felicity Powell
With contributions from Craig Fees and Fred Coldicott

LAST NAMES OF PEOPLE (or animals) ARE IN CAPITALS,
Buildings and Places are Capitalised, and
objects, businesses, organisations and topics are in italics.

108

109

112

113

114

118

119

120